MICROTOPIA

Midge Turing

Edited by
Stephen Barnwell

Antarctica Arts
MMXXIII

Coloring Books from Antarctica Arts
Cirque Fantastique
Living Fractals
Living Fractals 2
Living Fractals 3
Microtopia
Microtopia 2
Equinox
Angelikon
DreamTime

Other Books from Antarctica Arts
Lost Journals of Phineas Finke
Ikonographica
Willoughby's World Of Wonder
Oneirognosis, the Art of Dreaming

Published by Antarctica Arts

www.AntarcticaArts.com

Copyright © 2023 Stephen Barnwell

All rights reserved. No part of this book may be used or reproduced in any form or by any means, mechanical or electronic, including photocopying and recording, or by any information storage and retrieval system, without written permission of the publisher.

ISBN 978-1-7339649-1-3

The illustrations in this book were created with the assistance of an Artificial Intelligence.

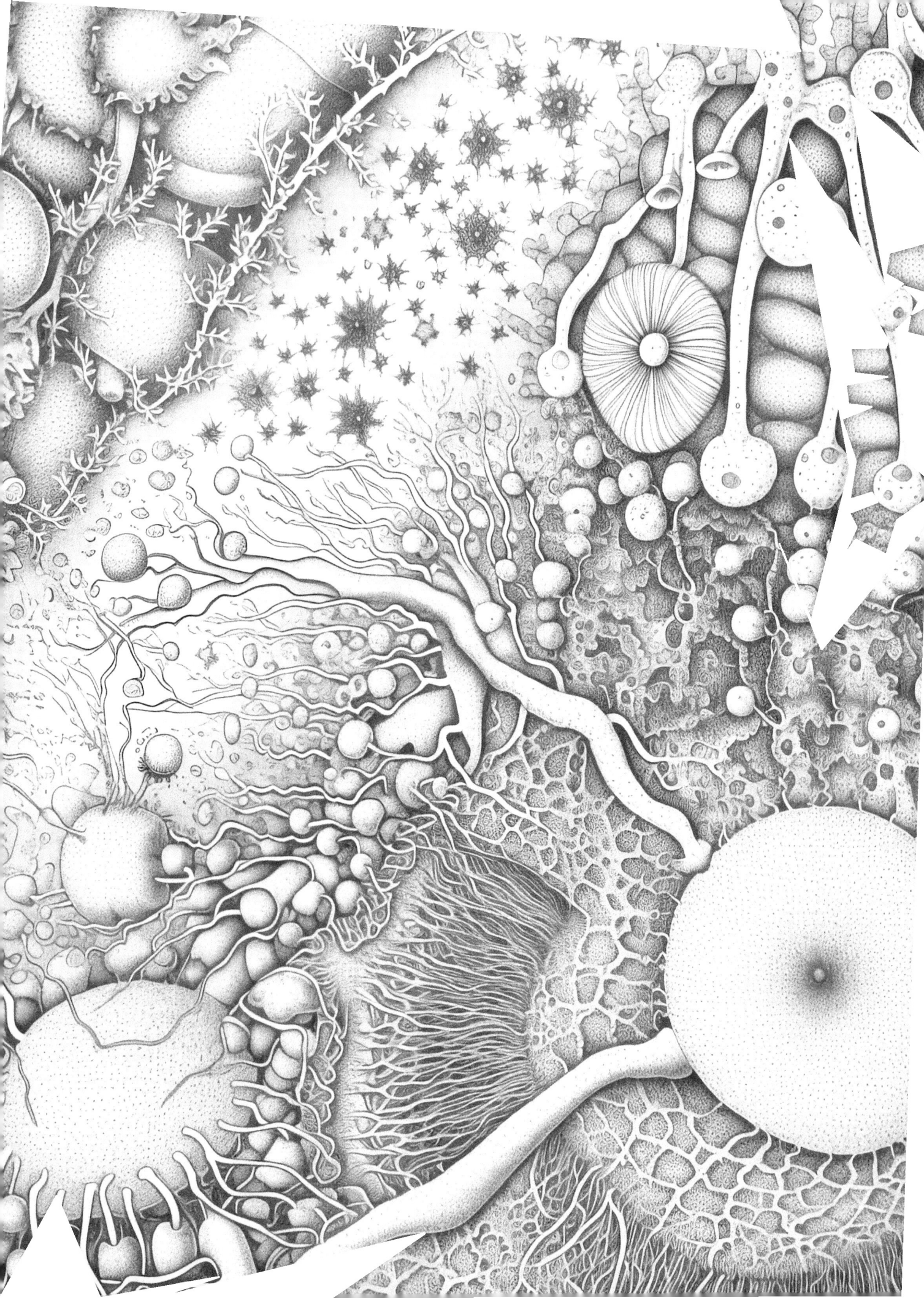

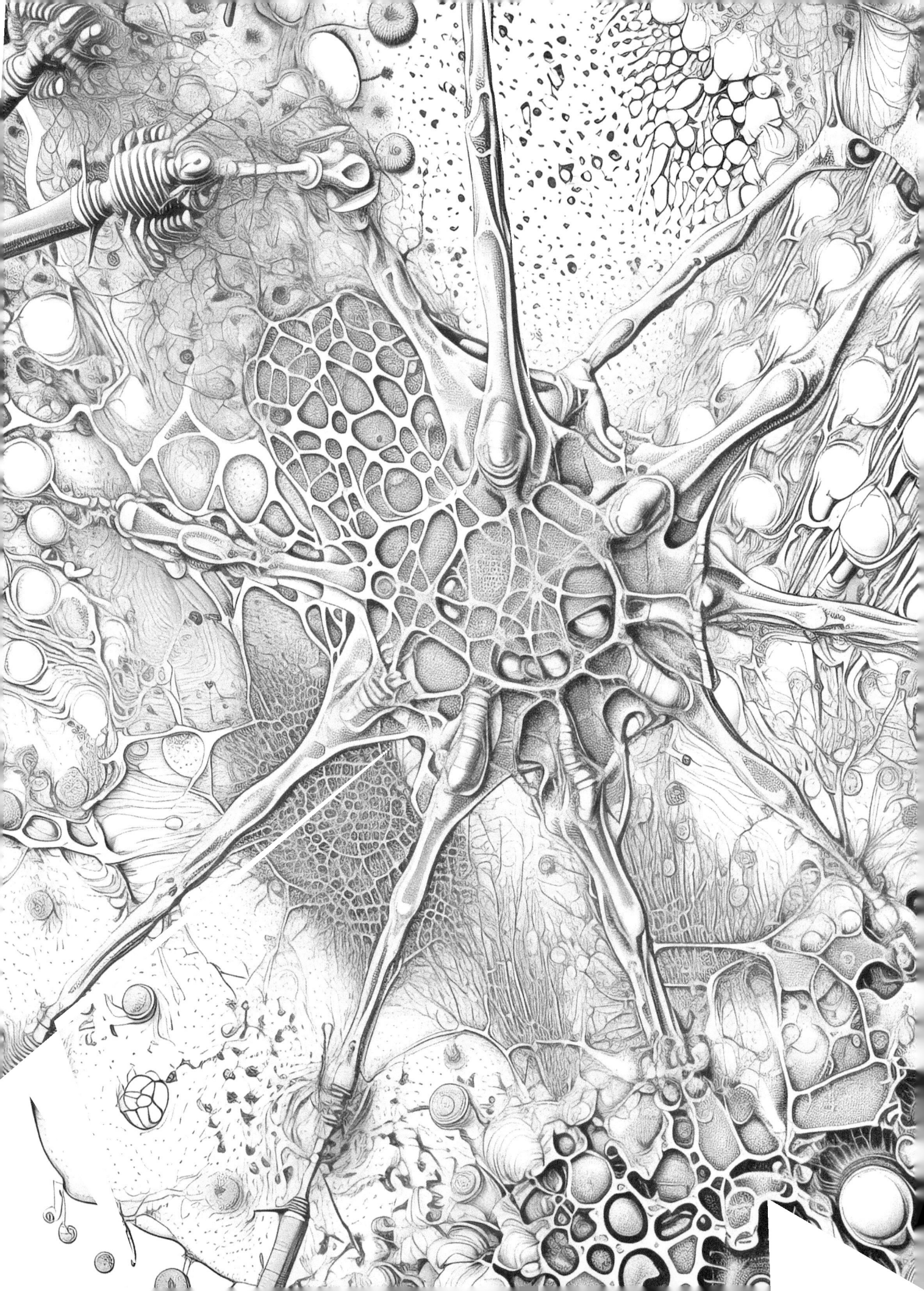

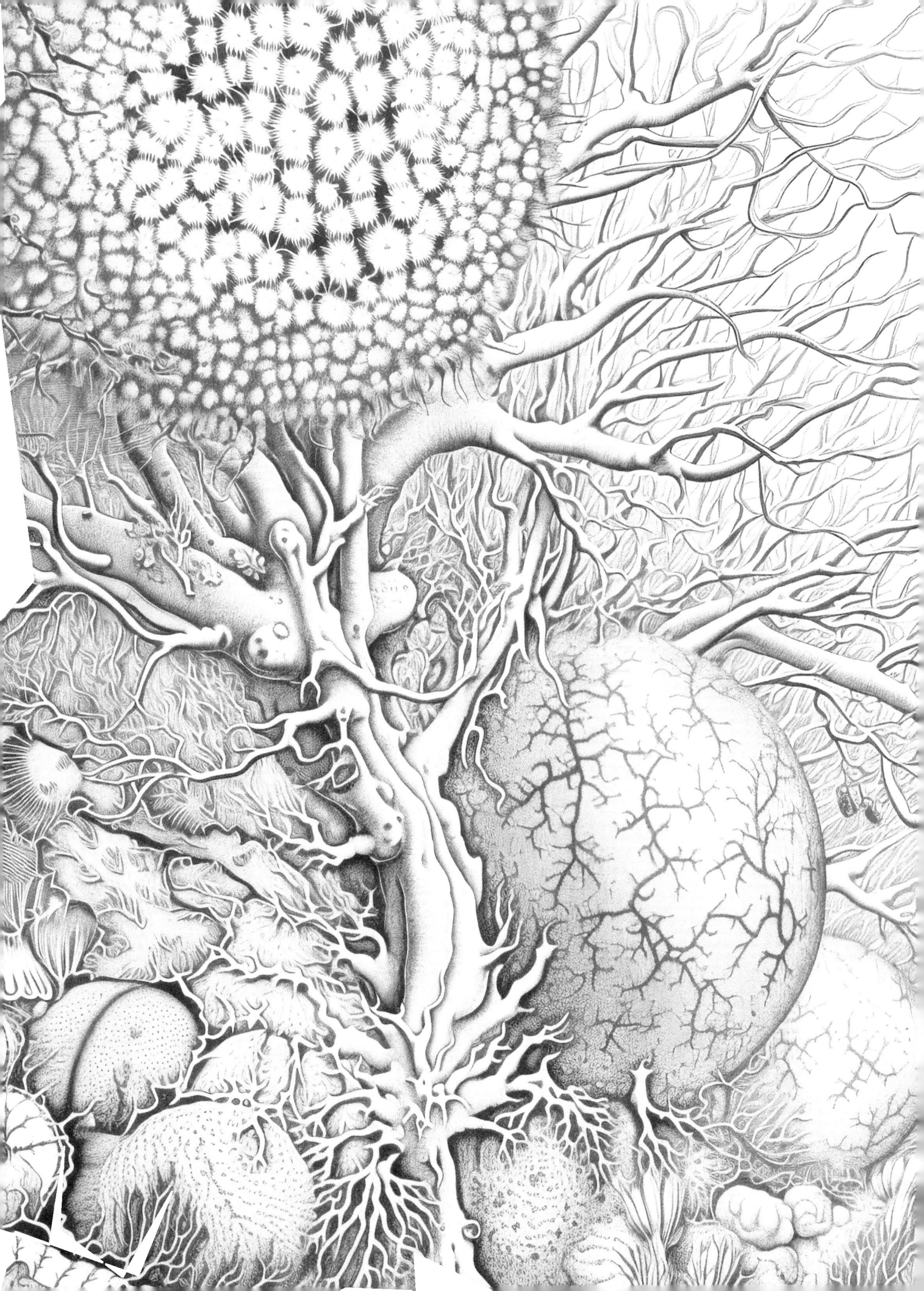

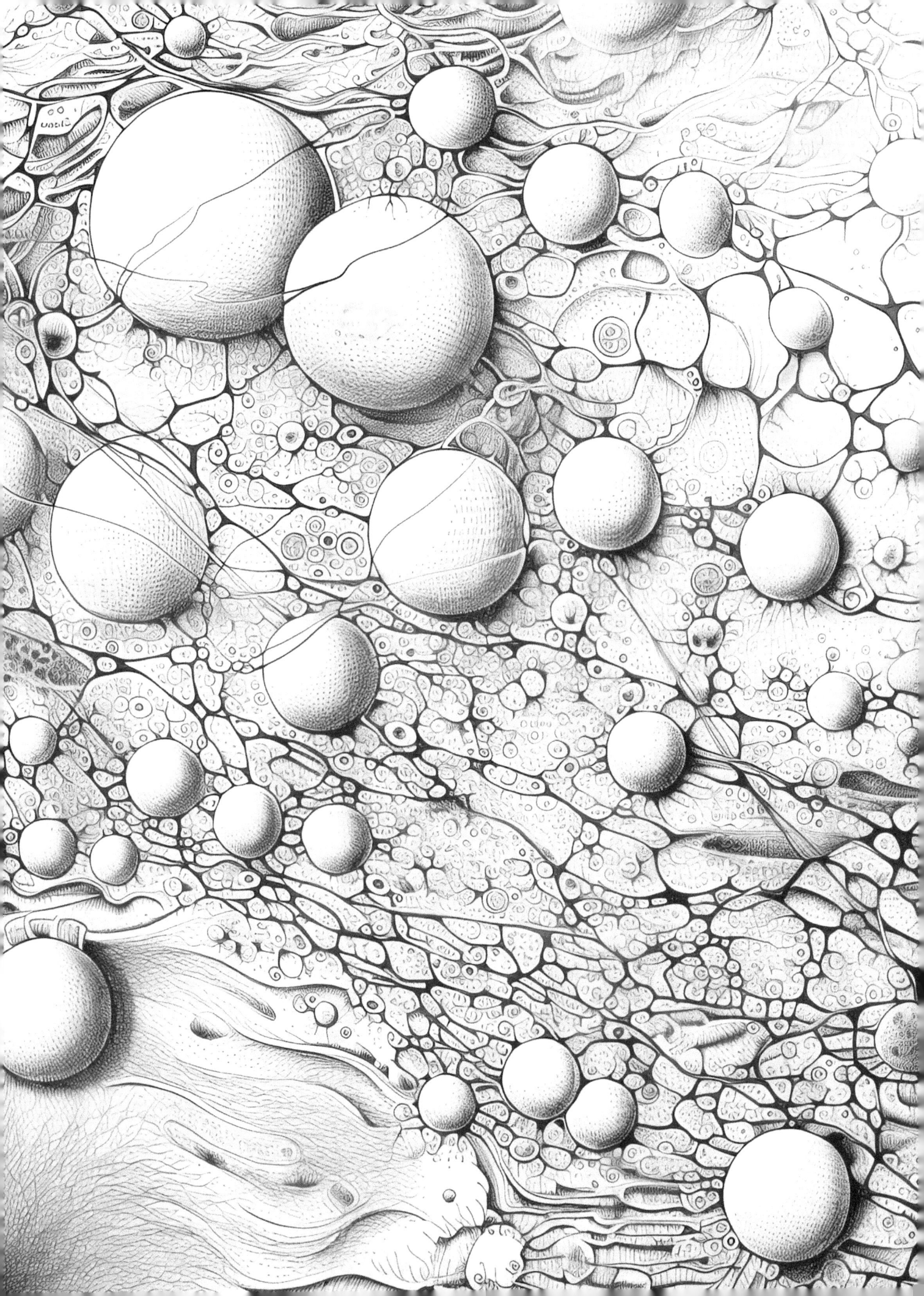

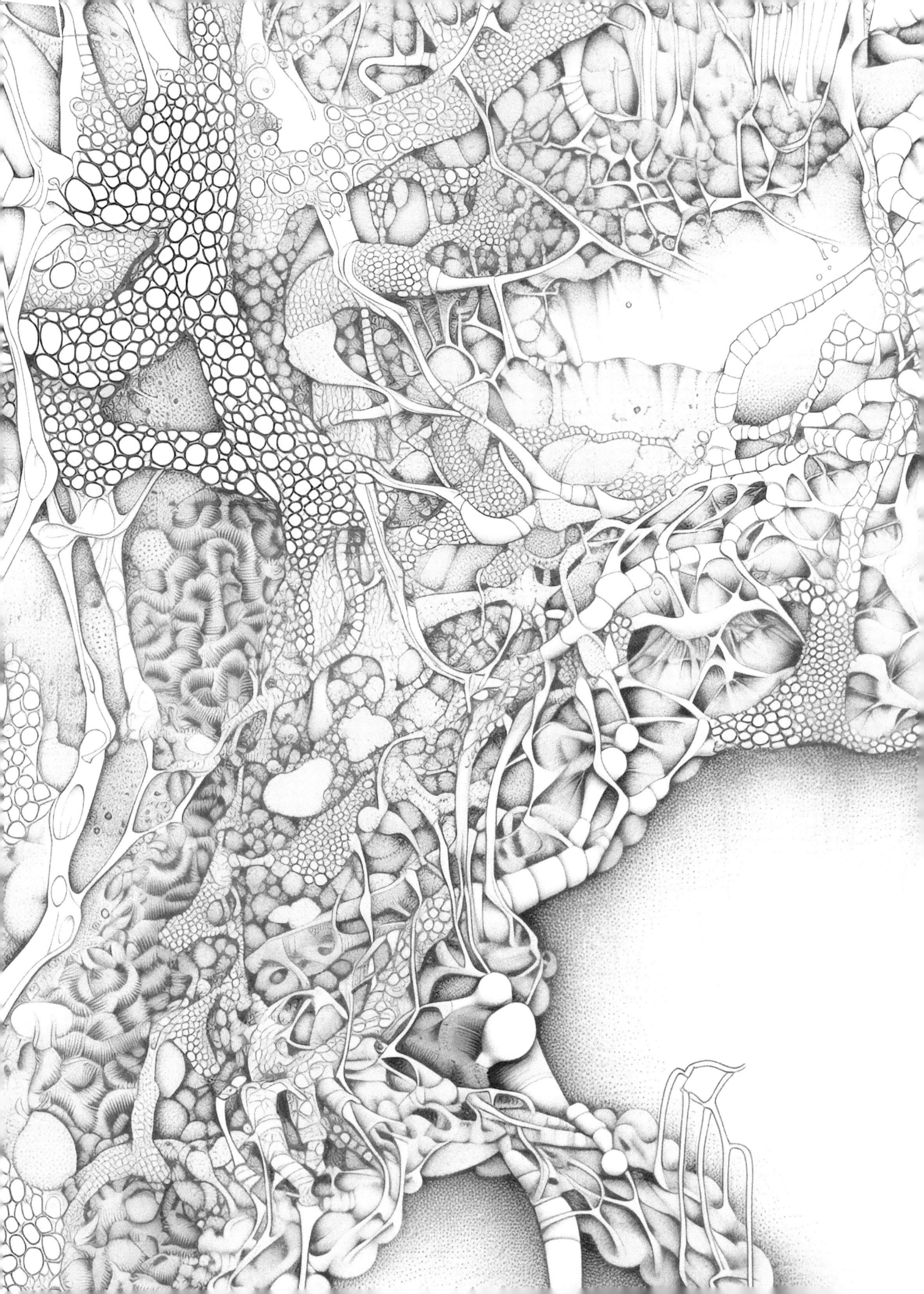

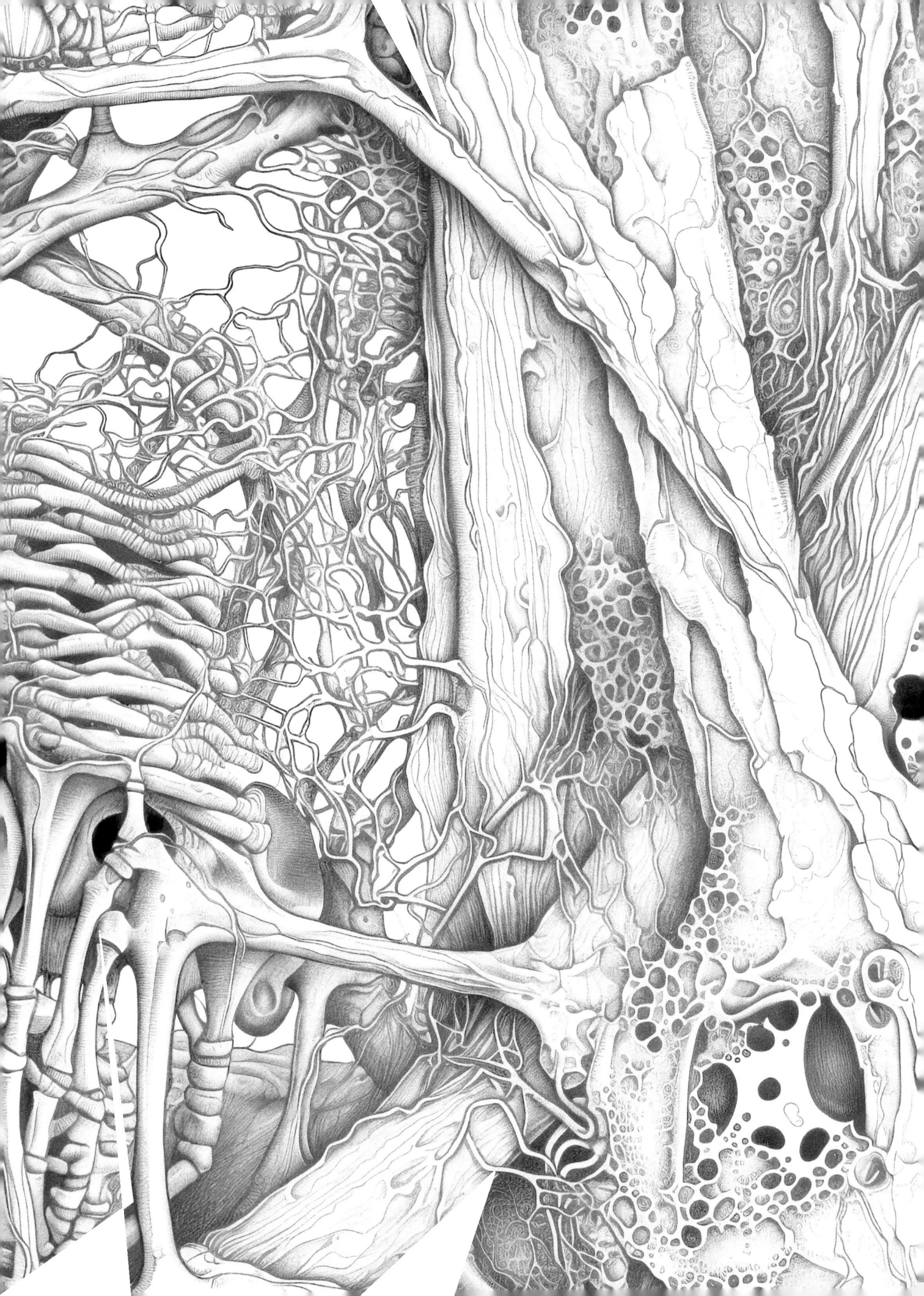

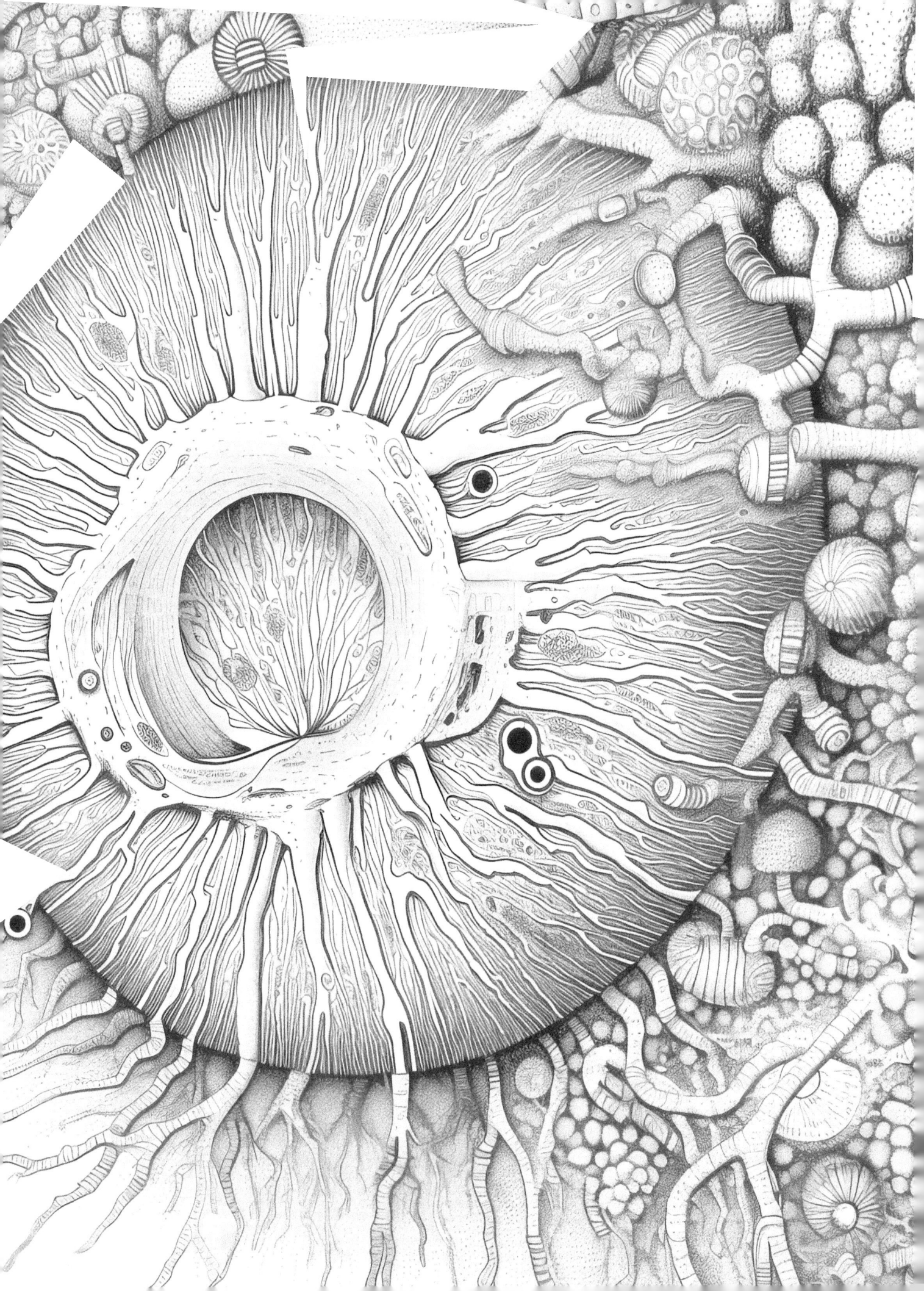

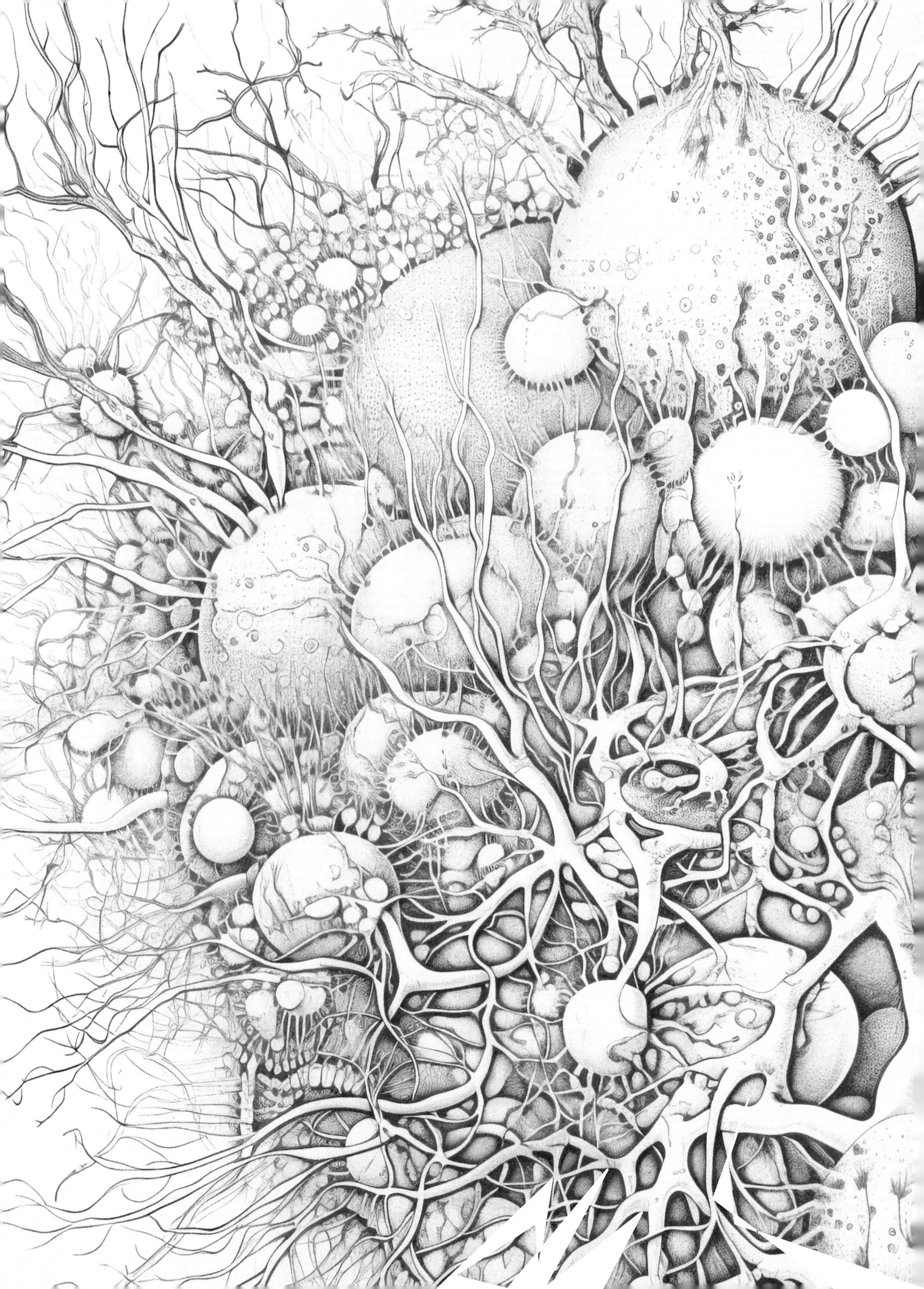

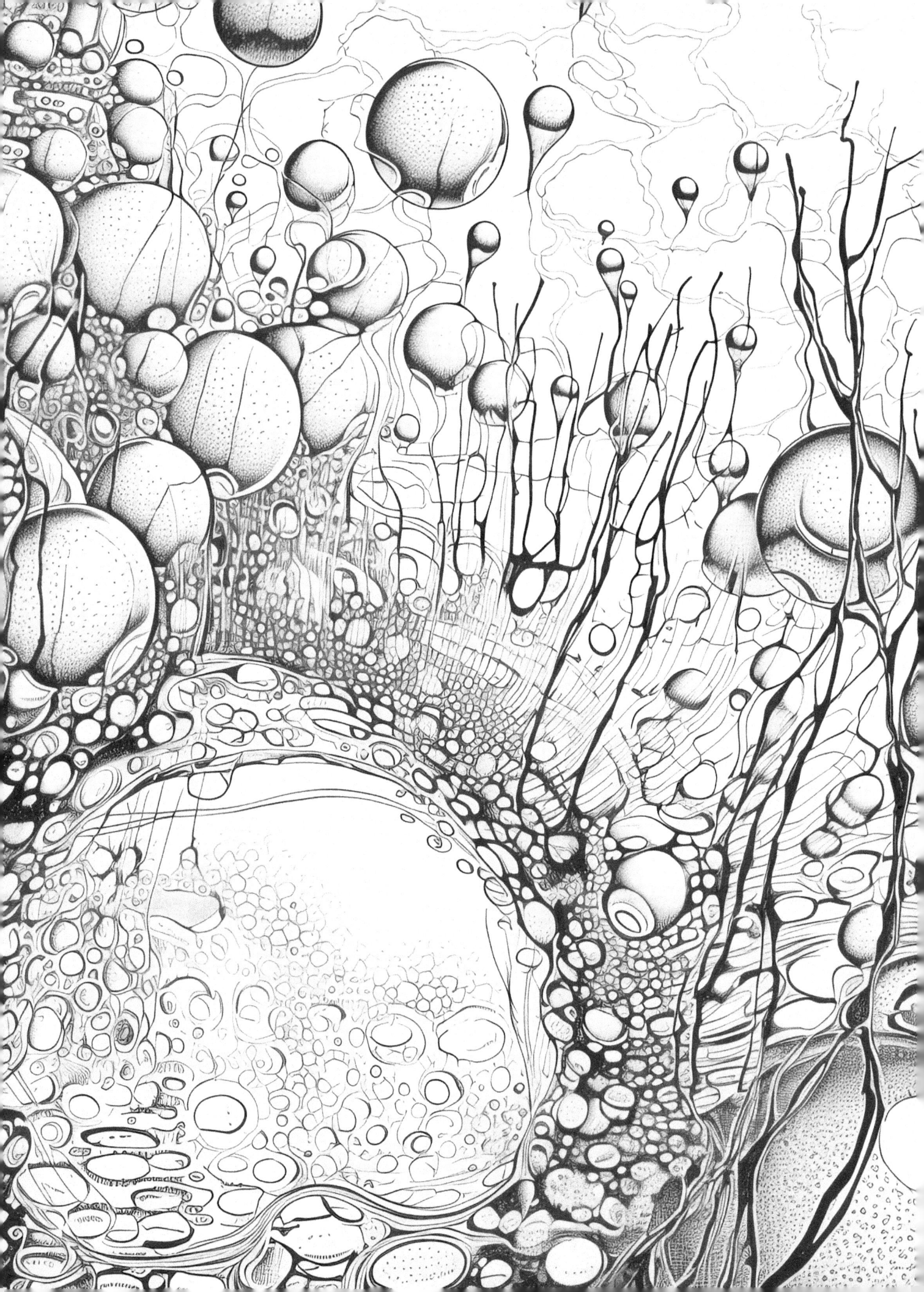

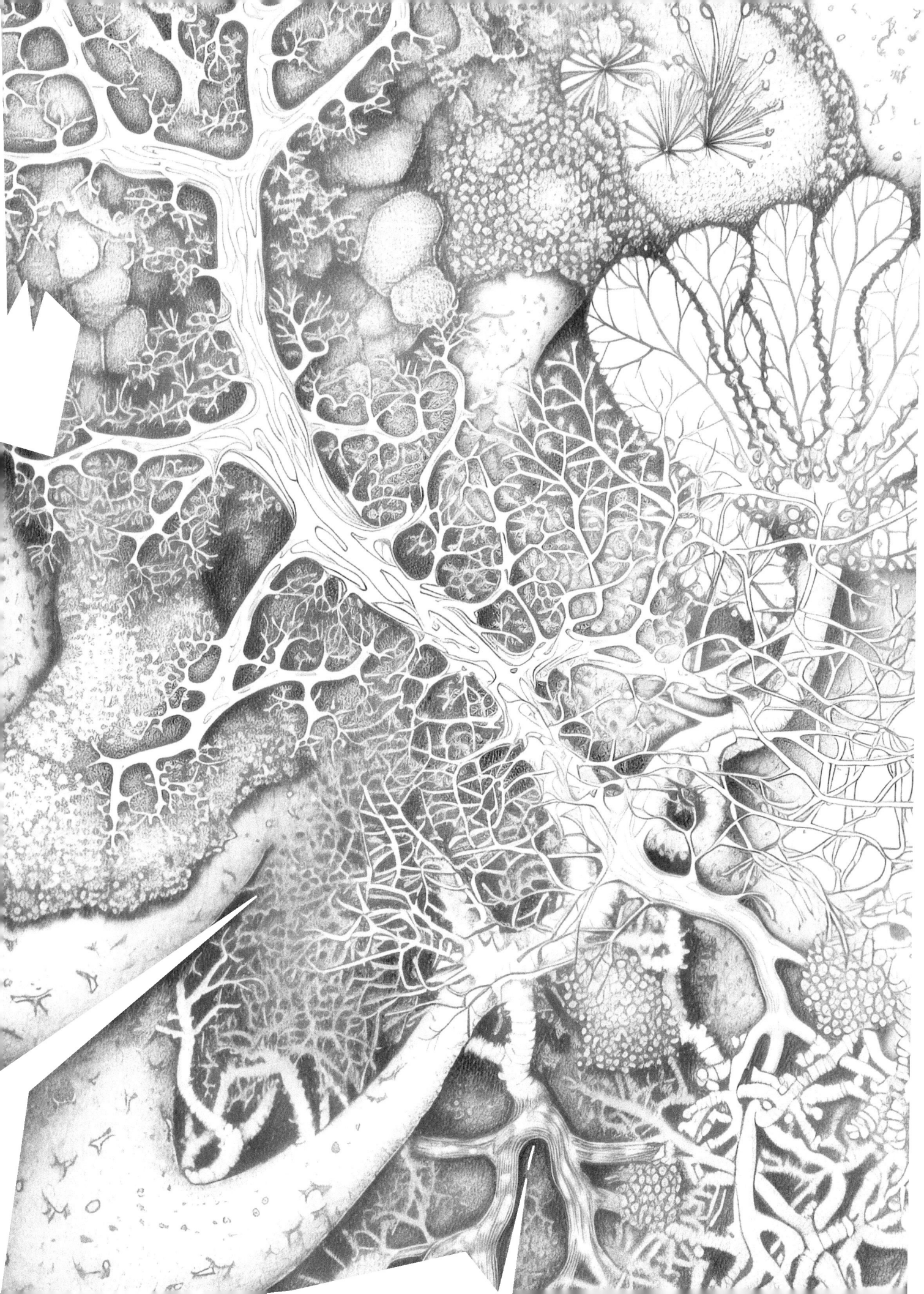

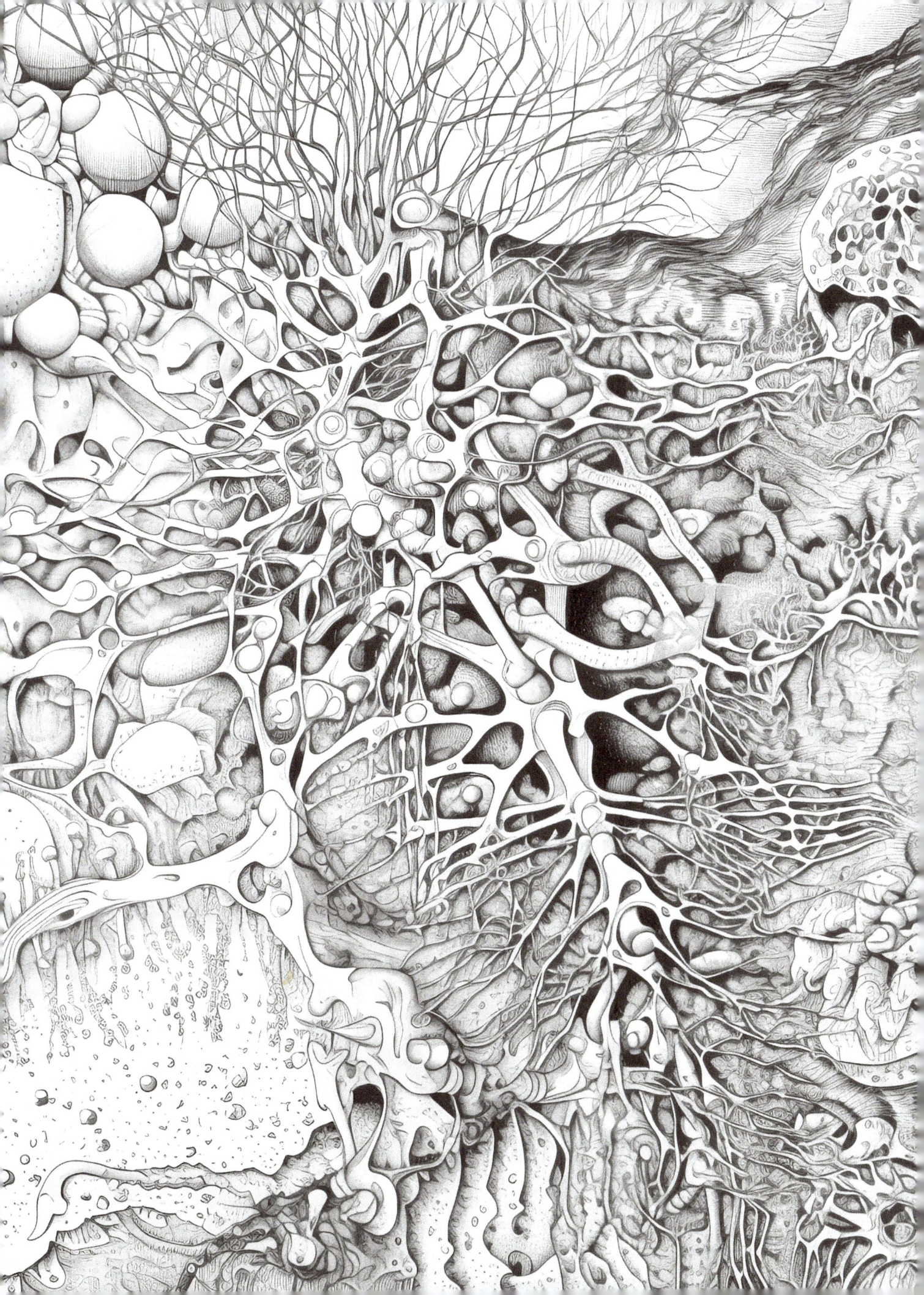

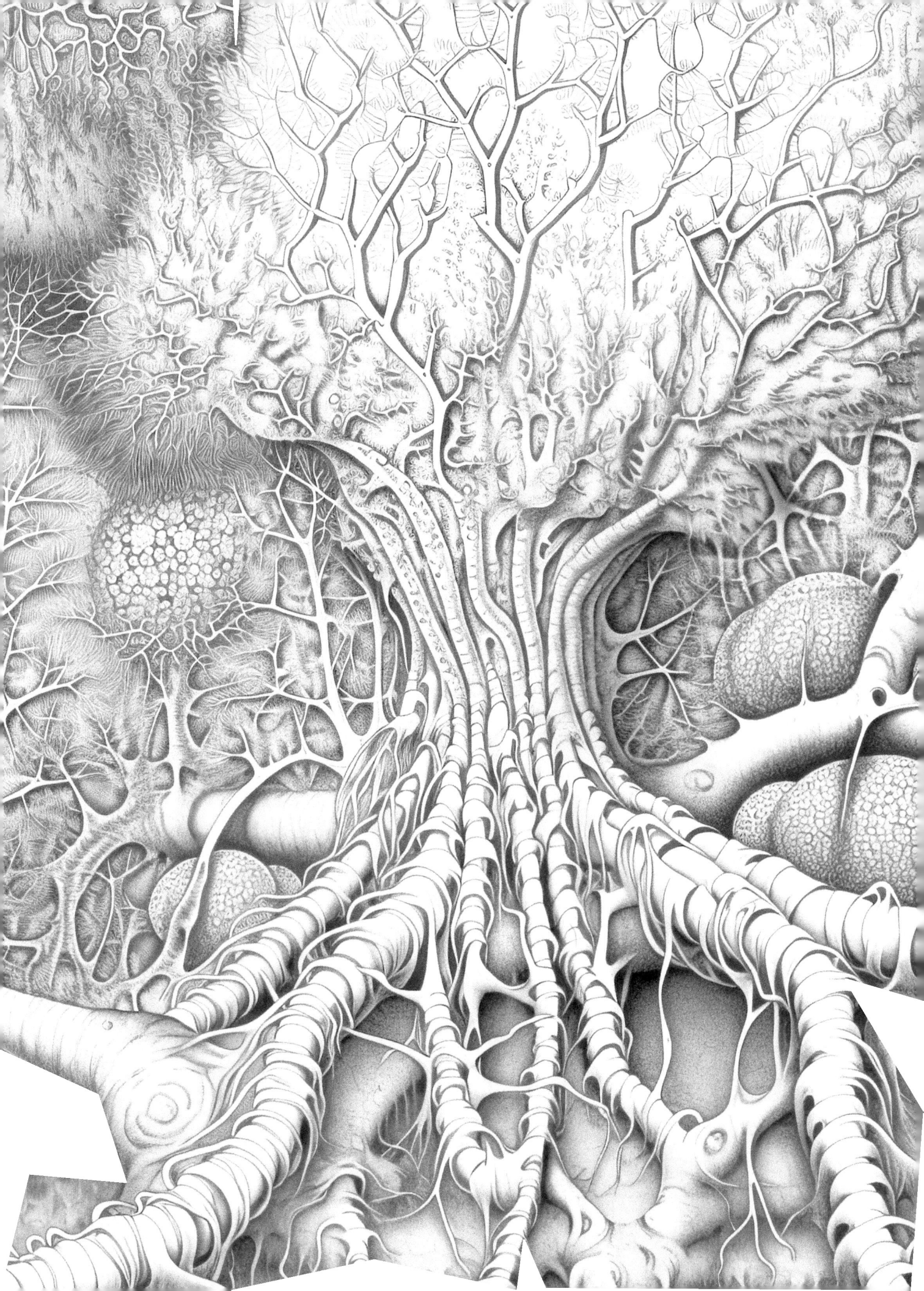

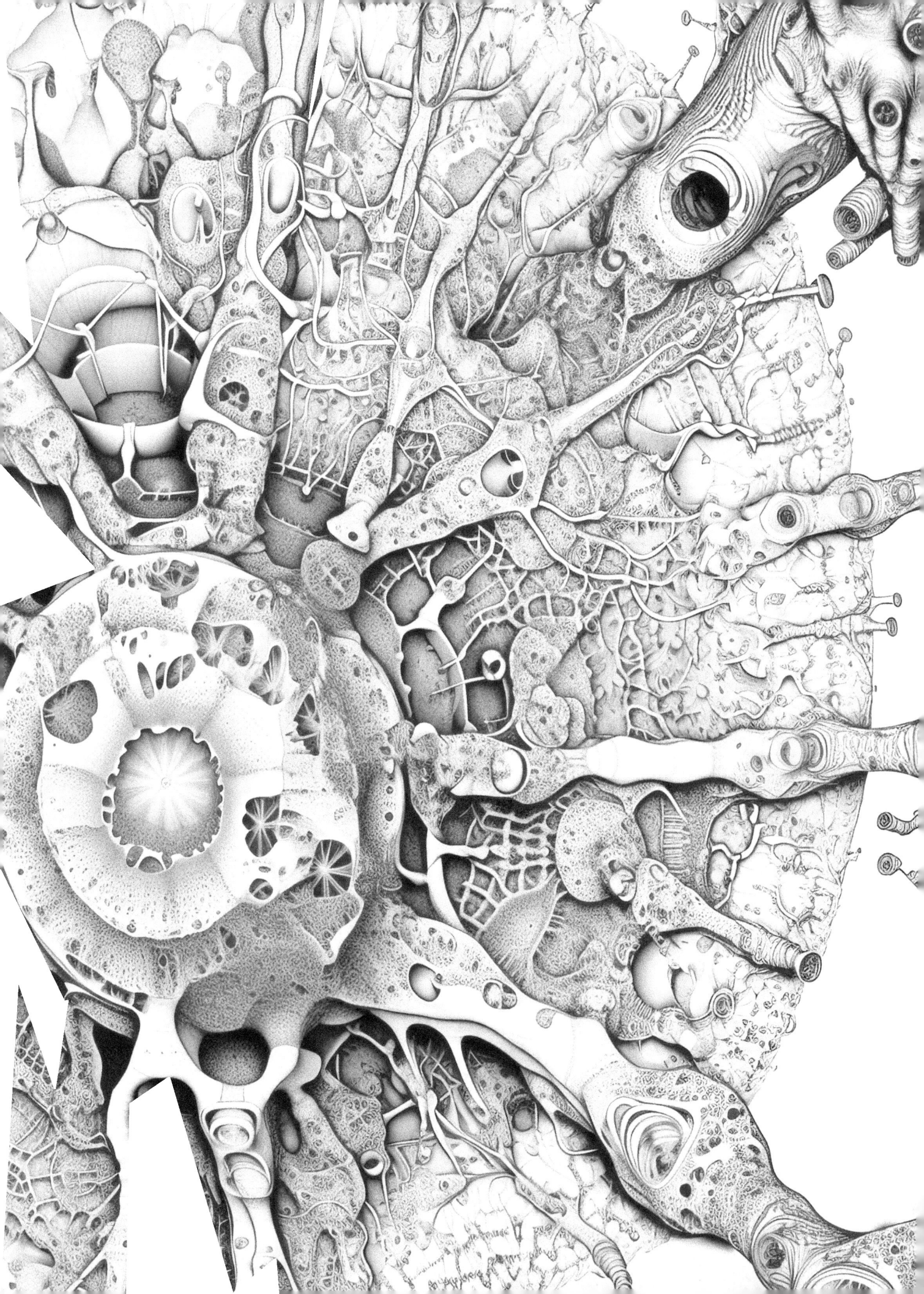

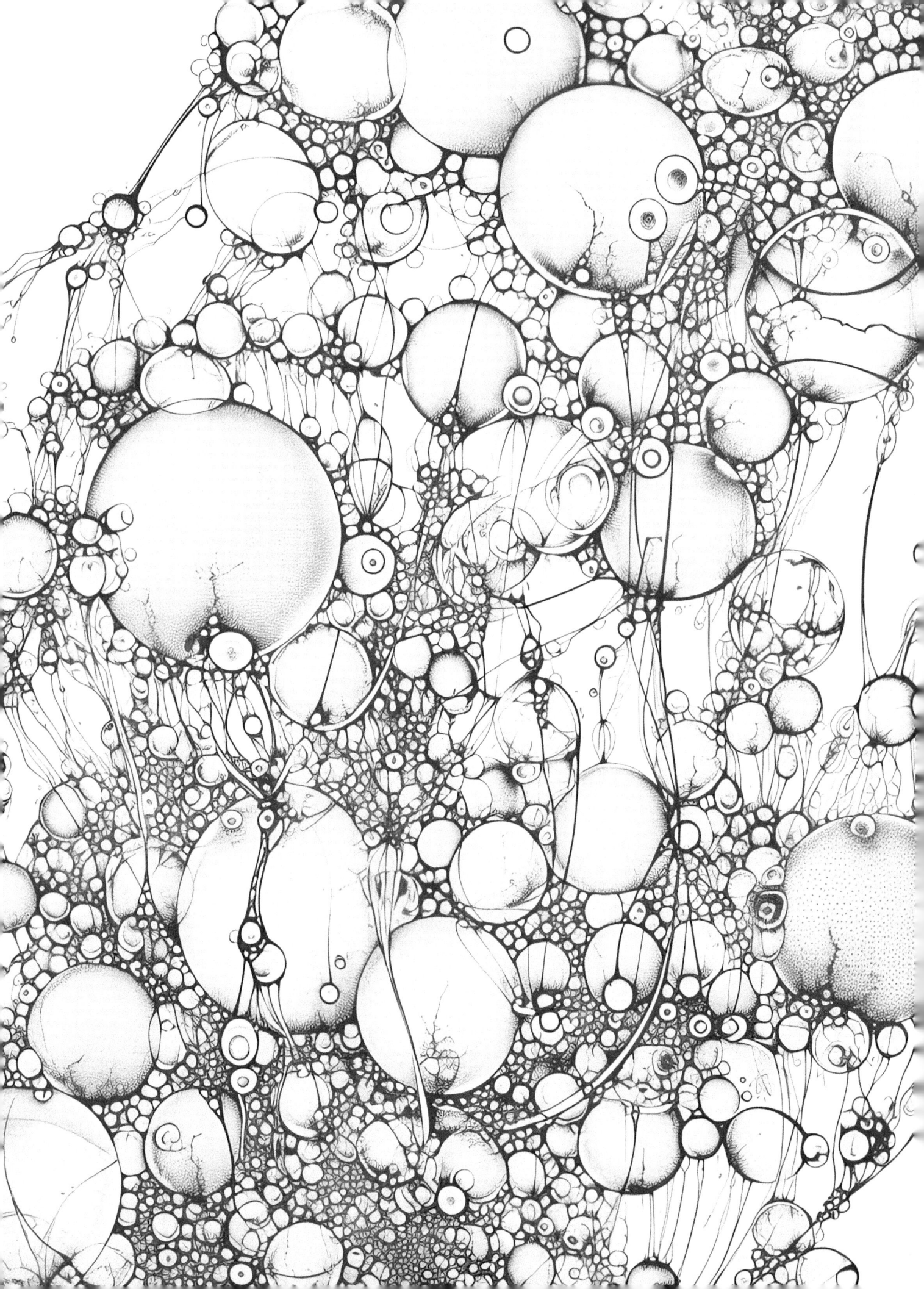

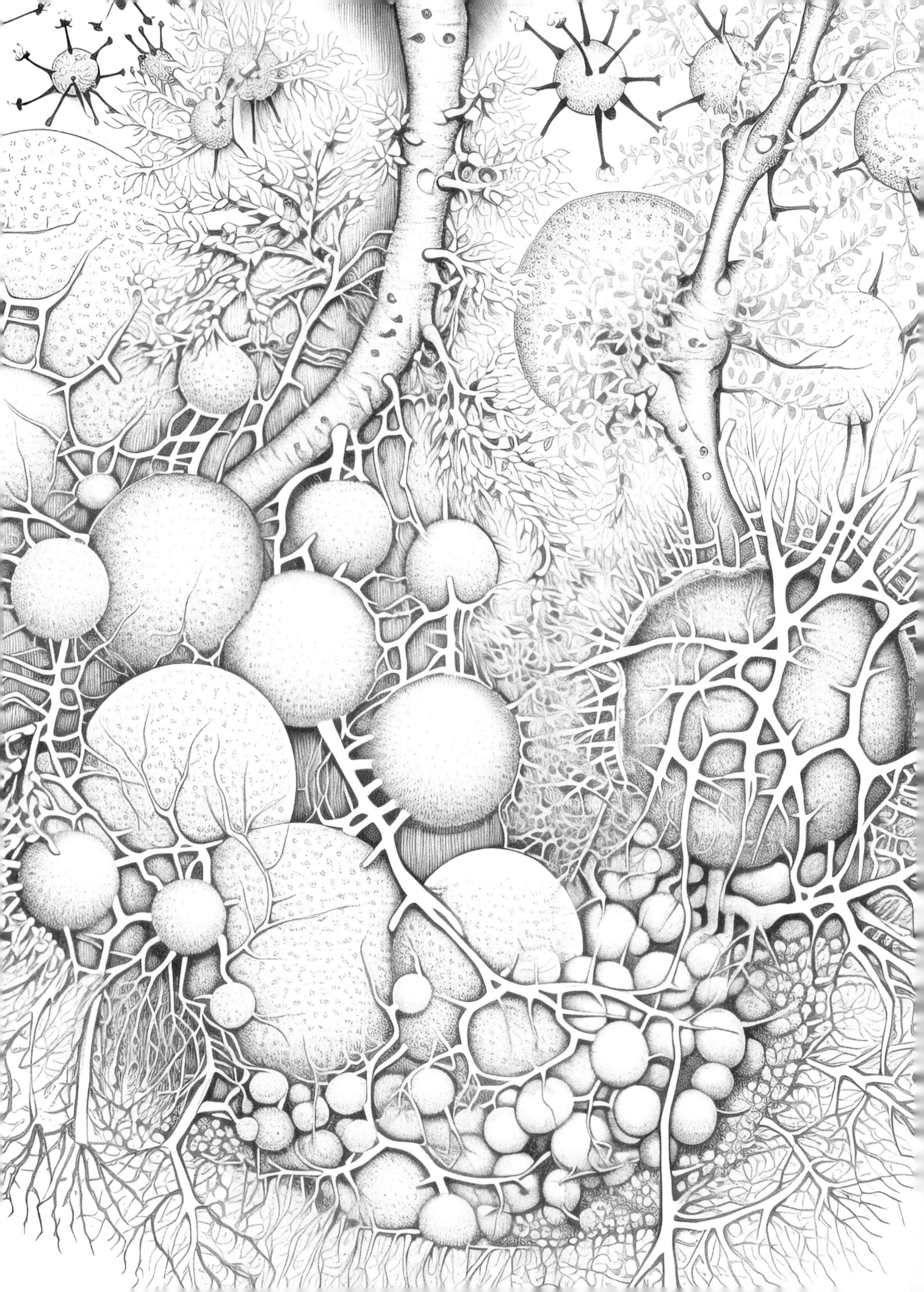

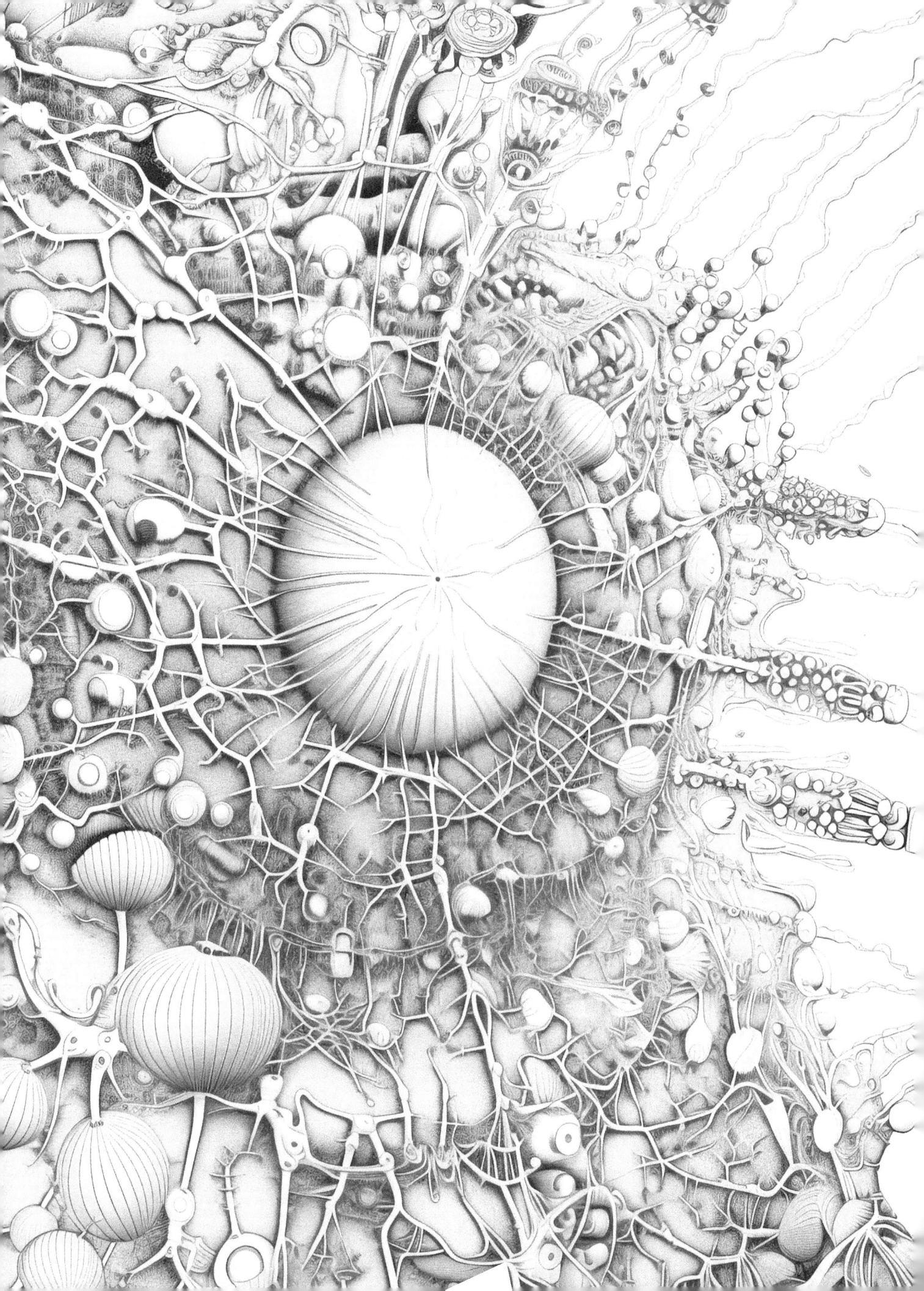

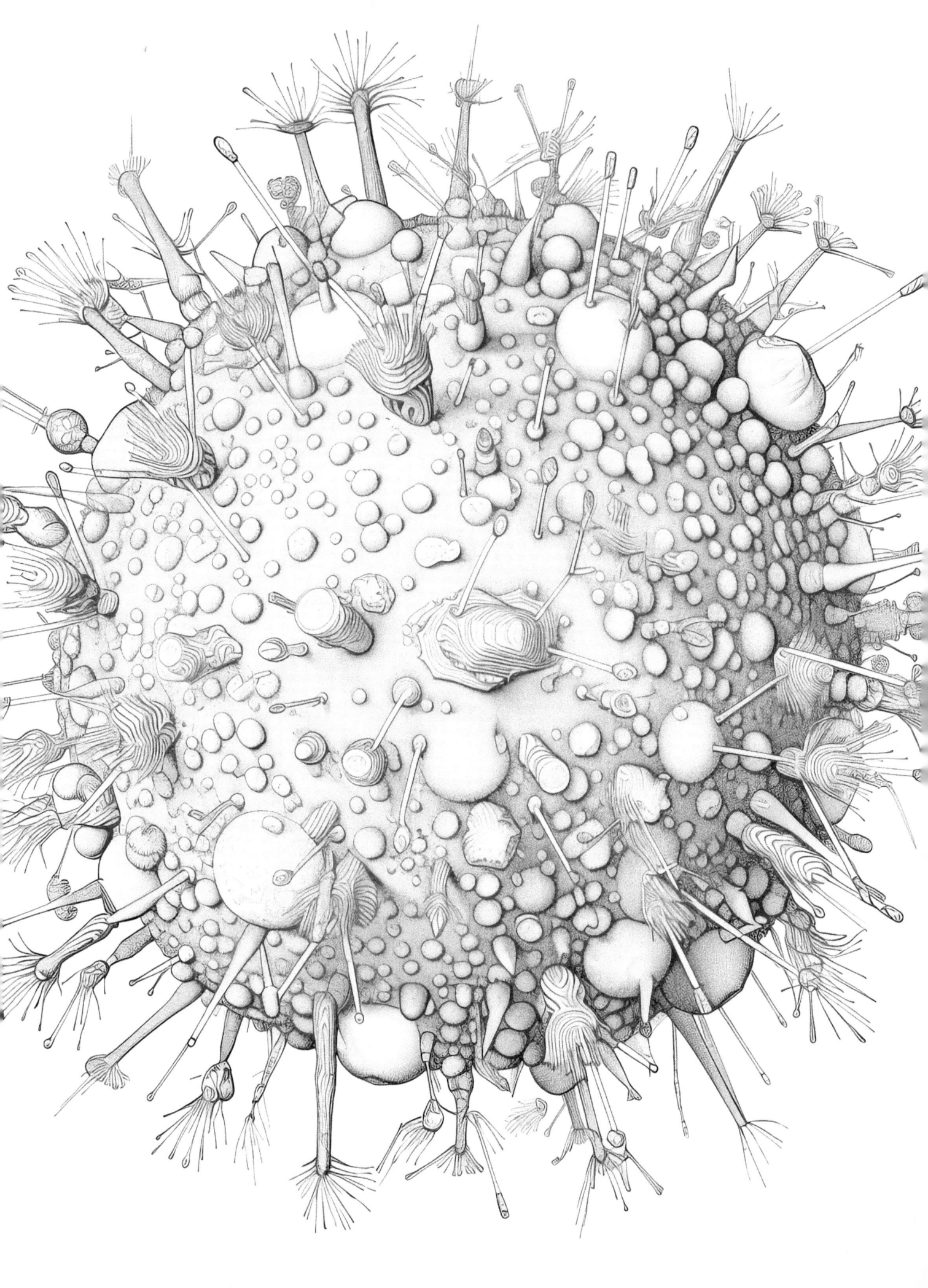

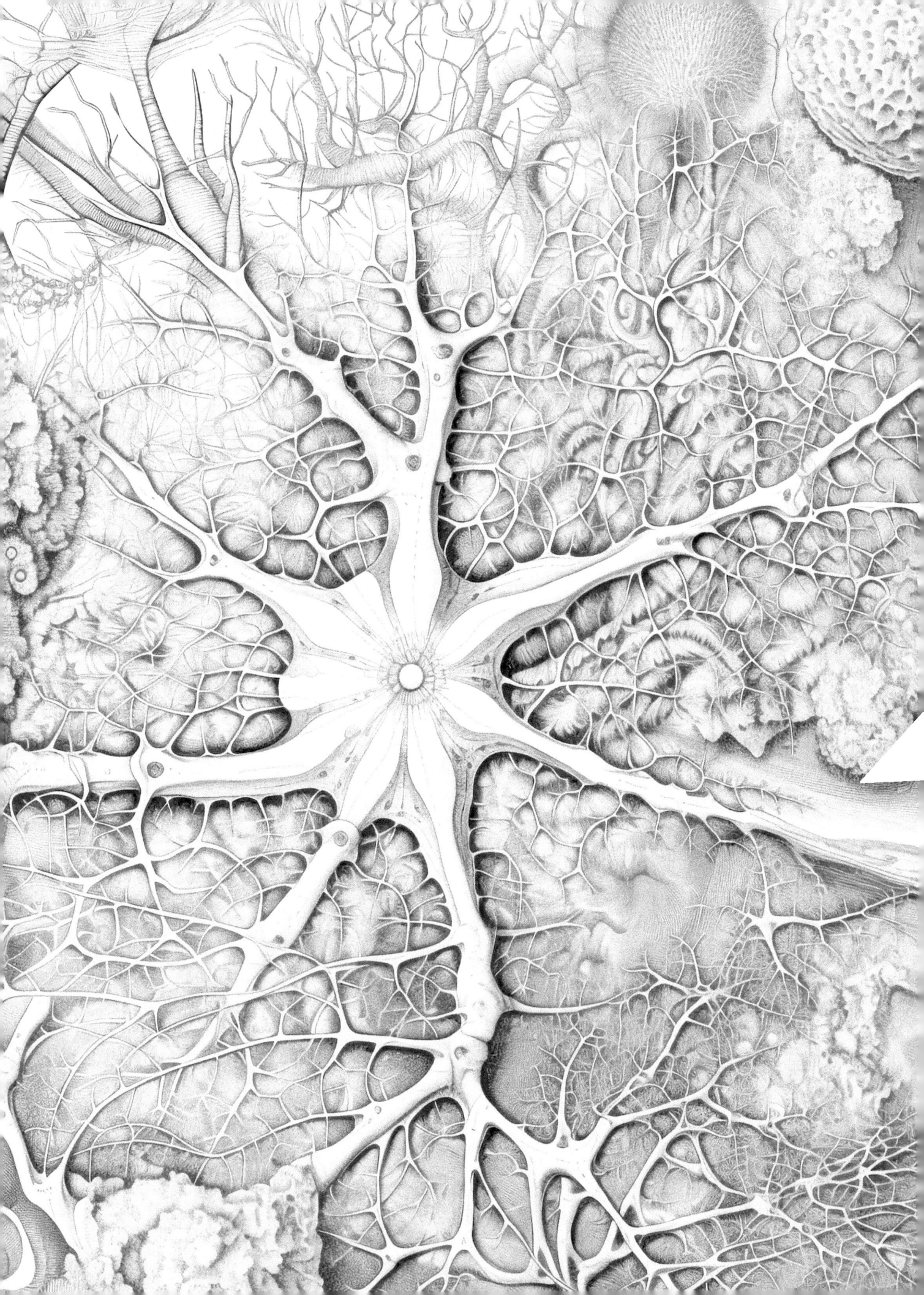

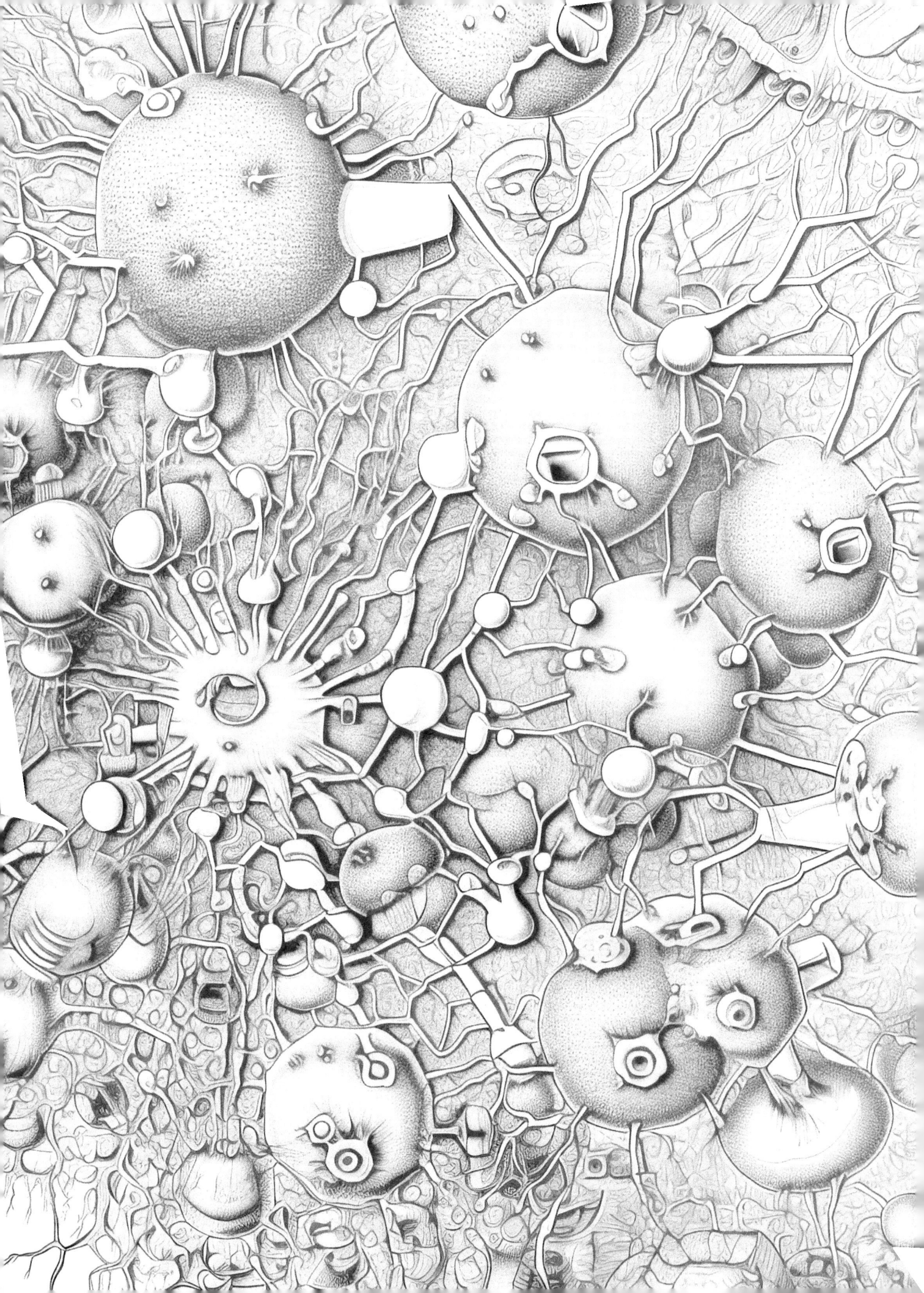

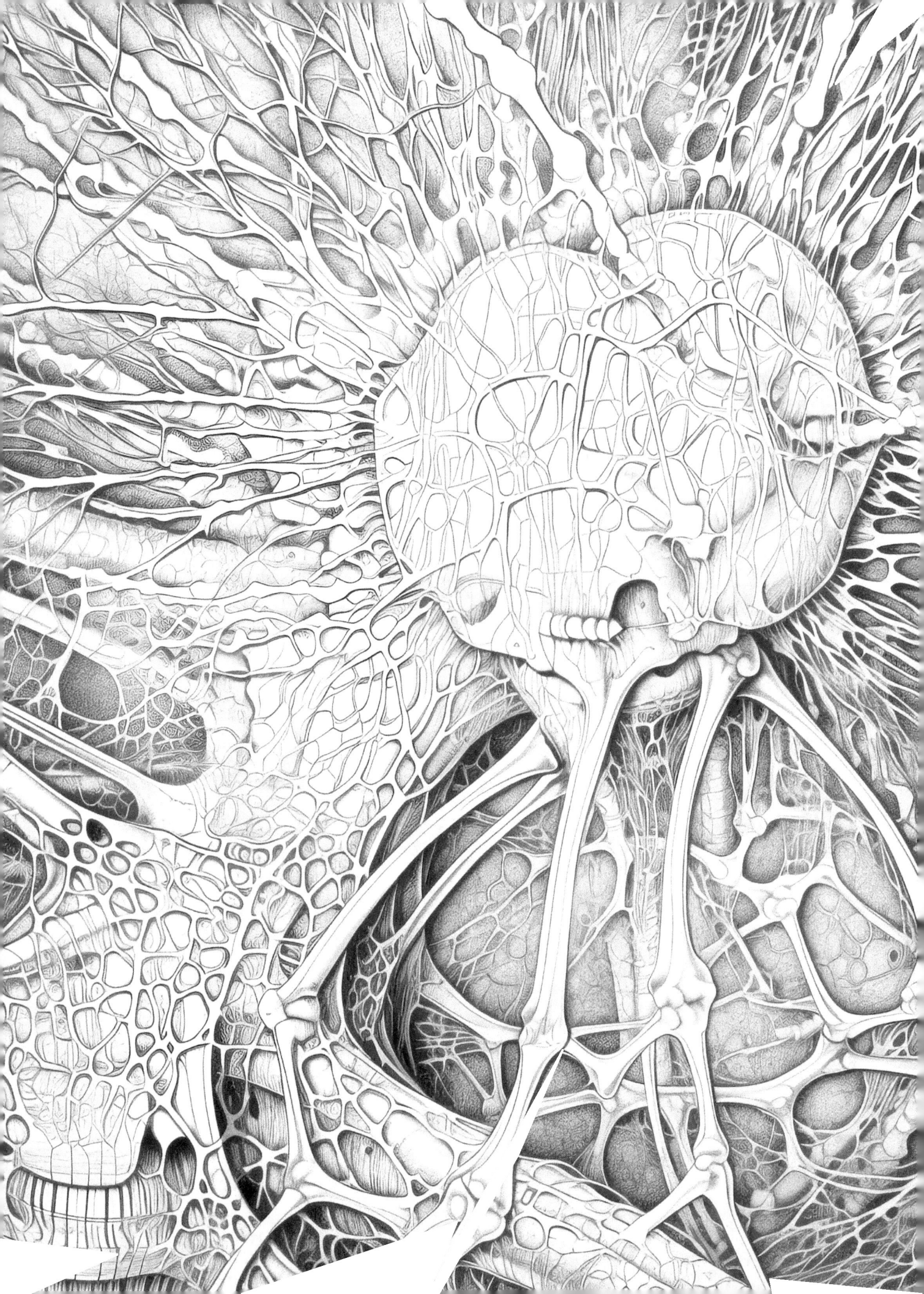

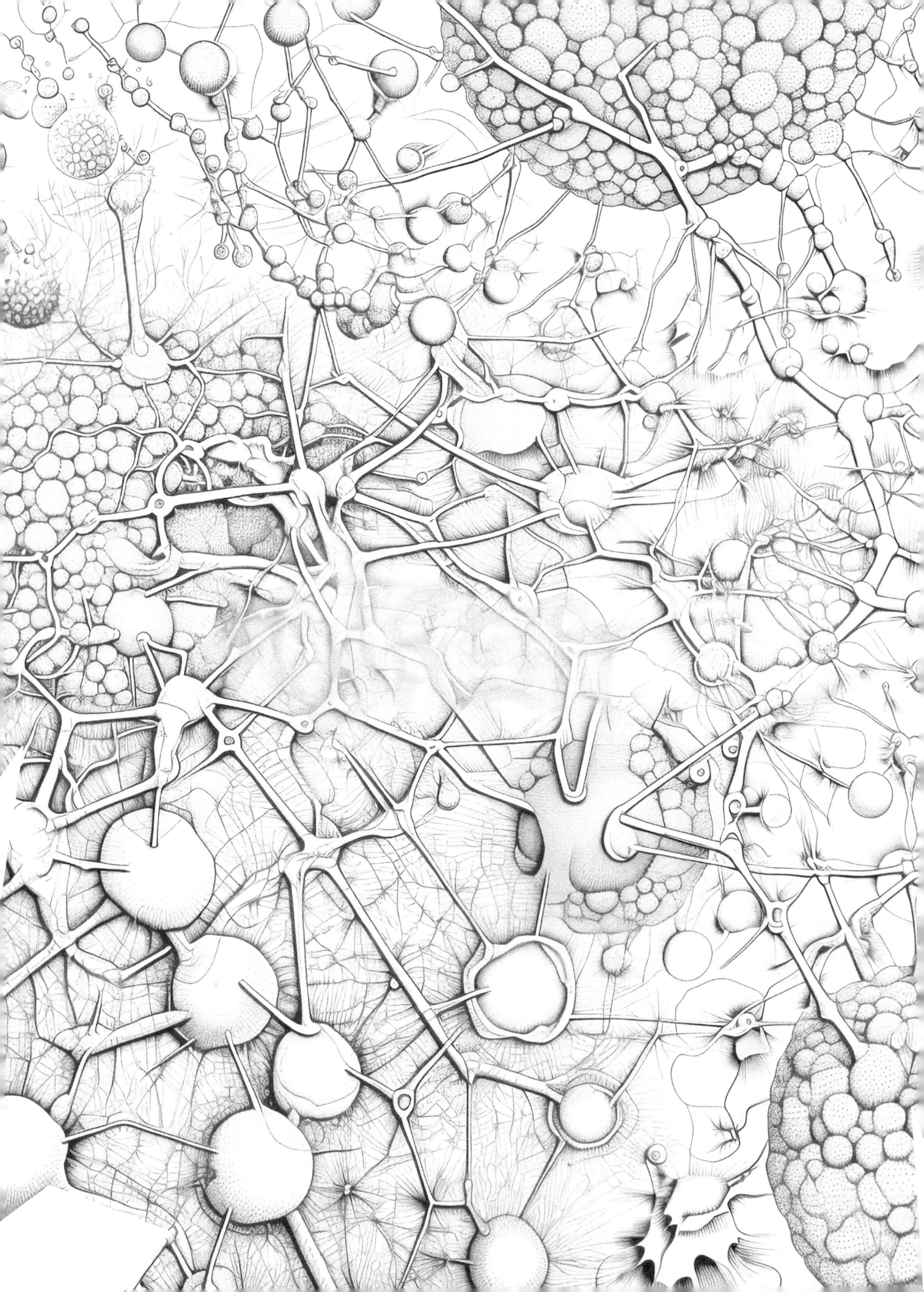

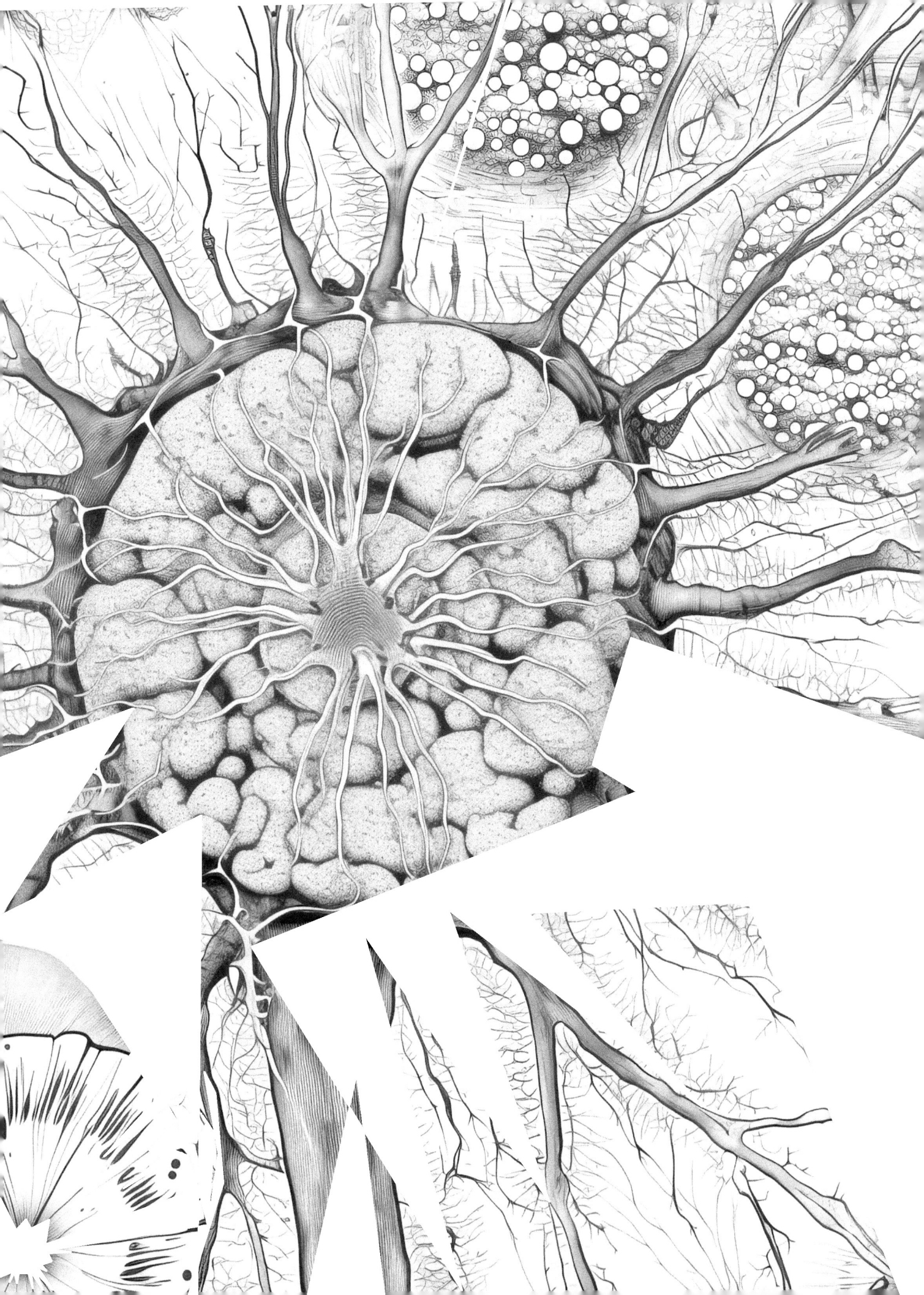

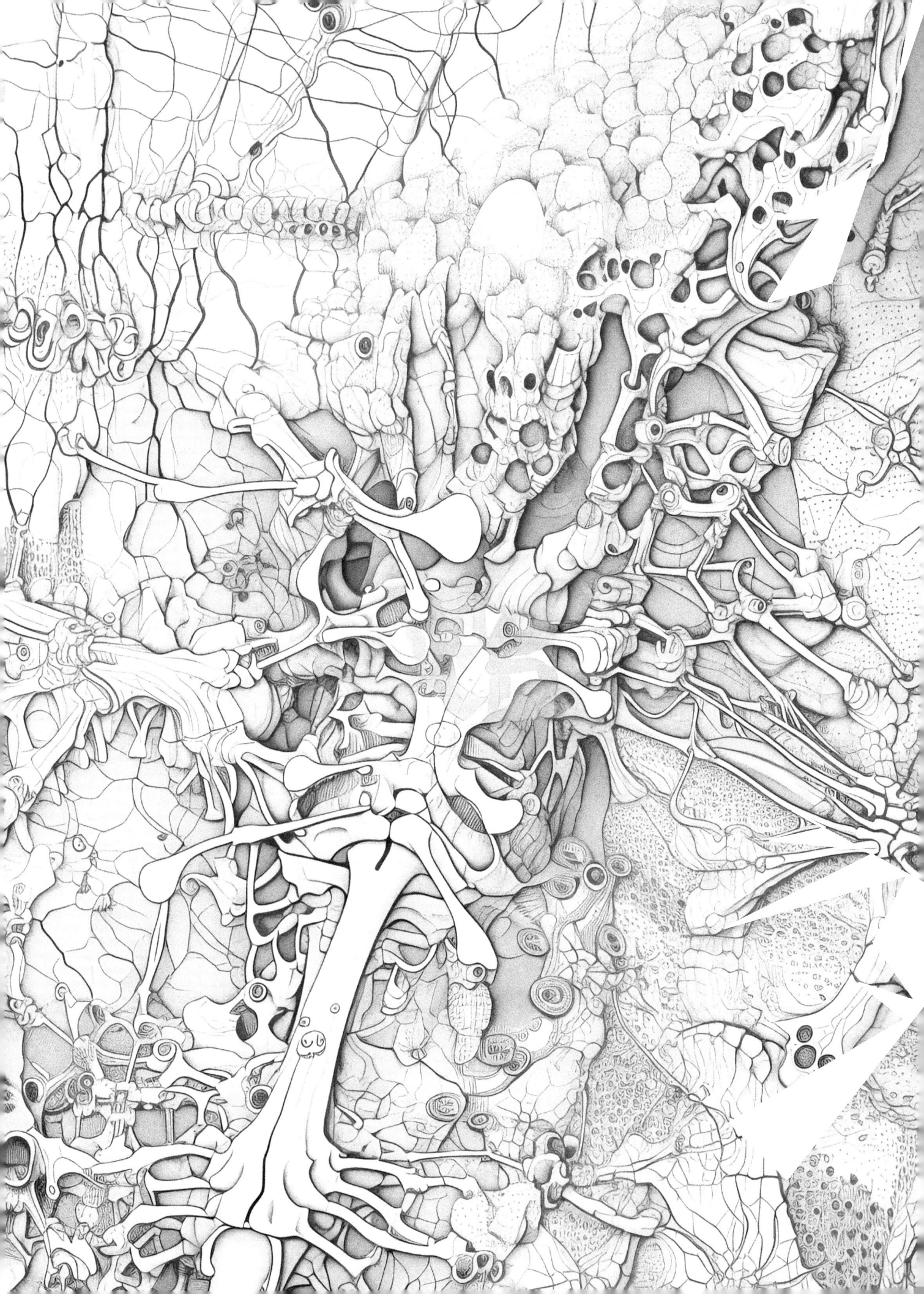

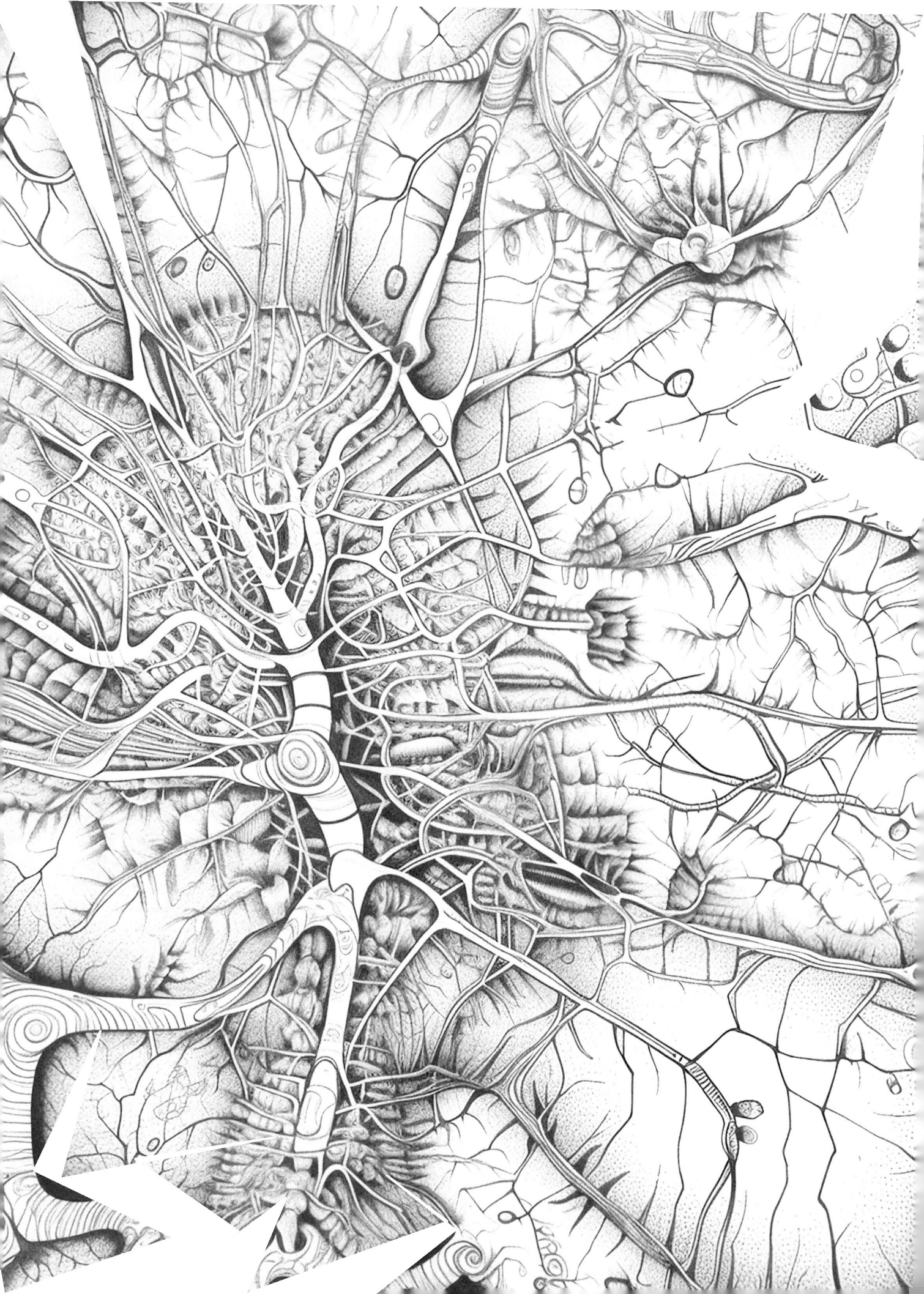

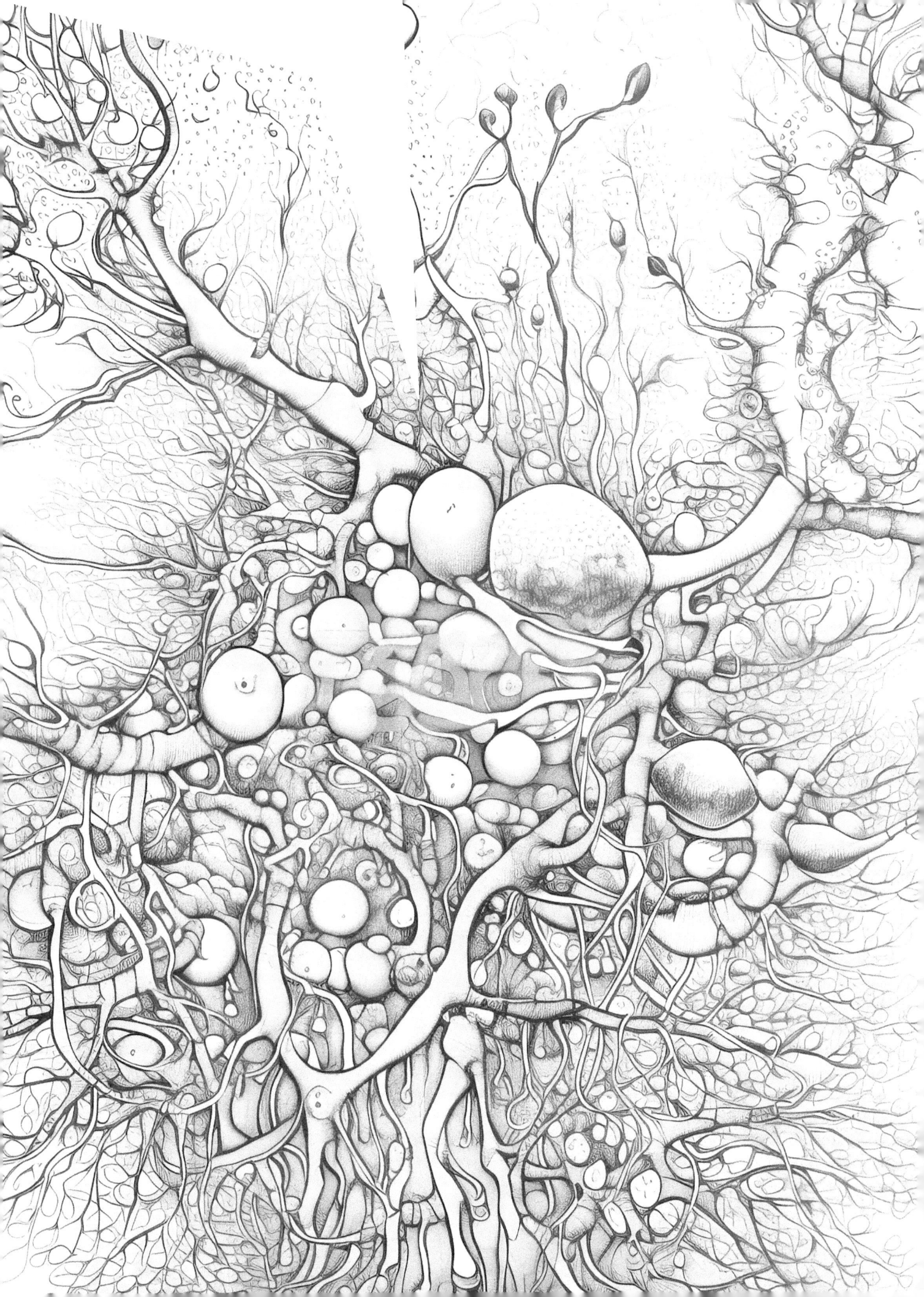

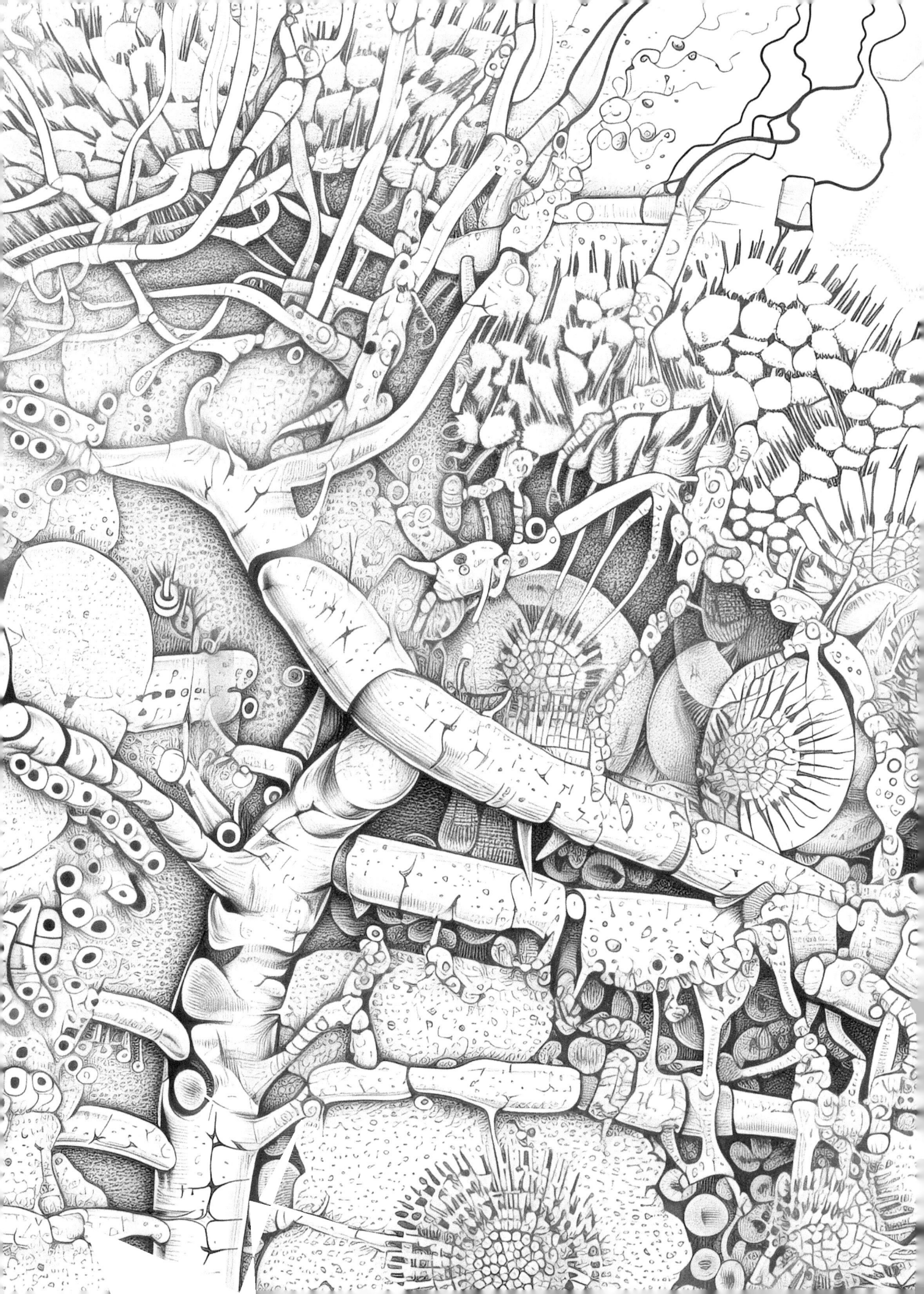

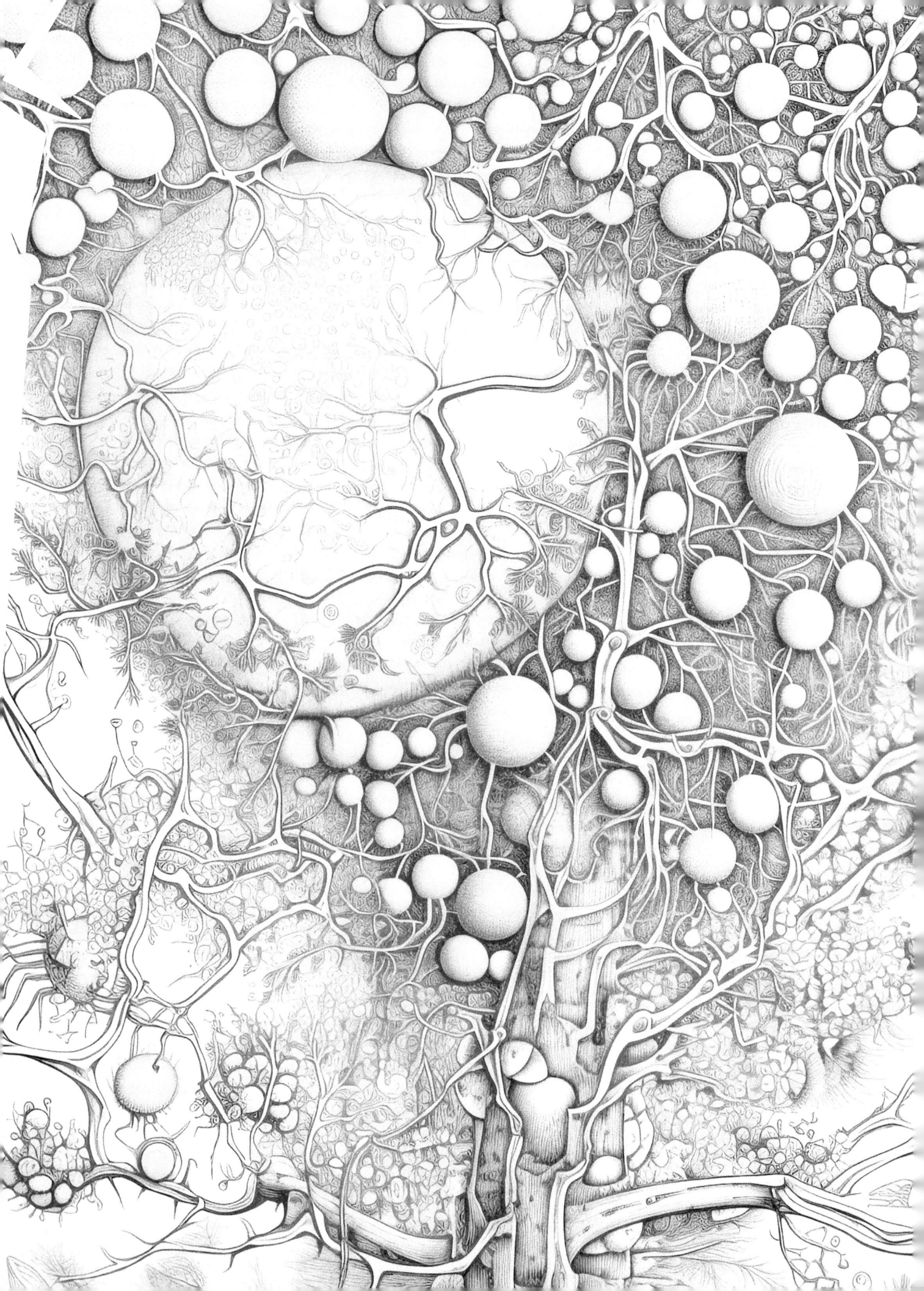

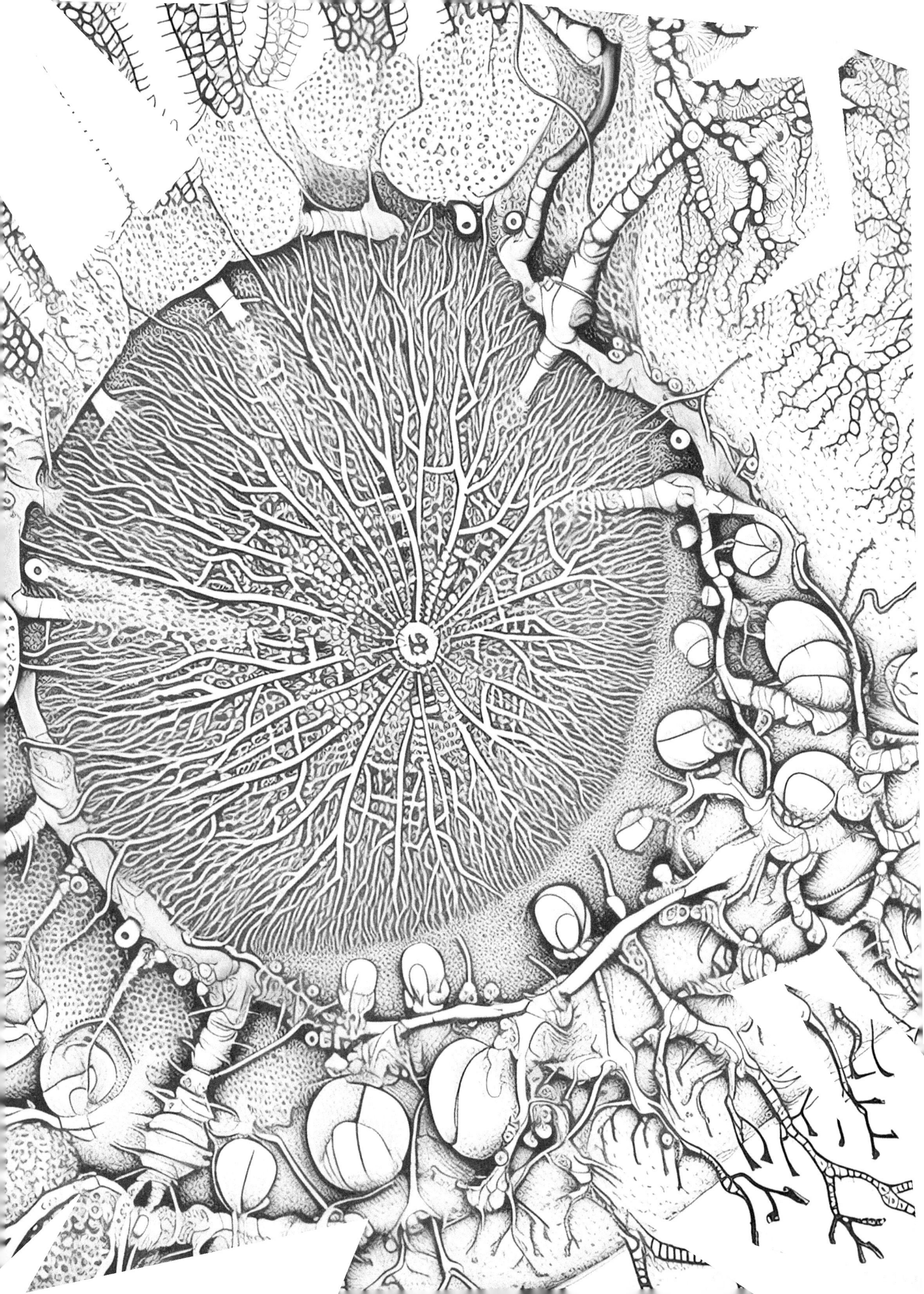

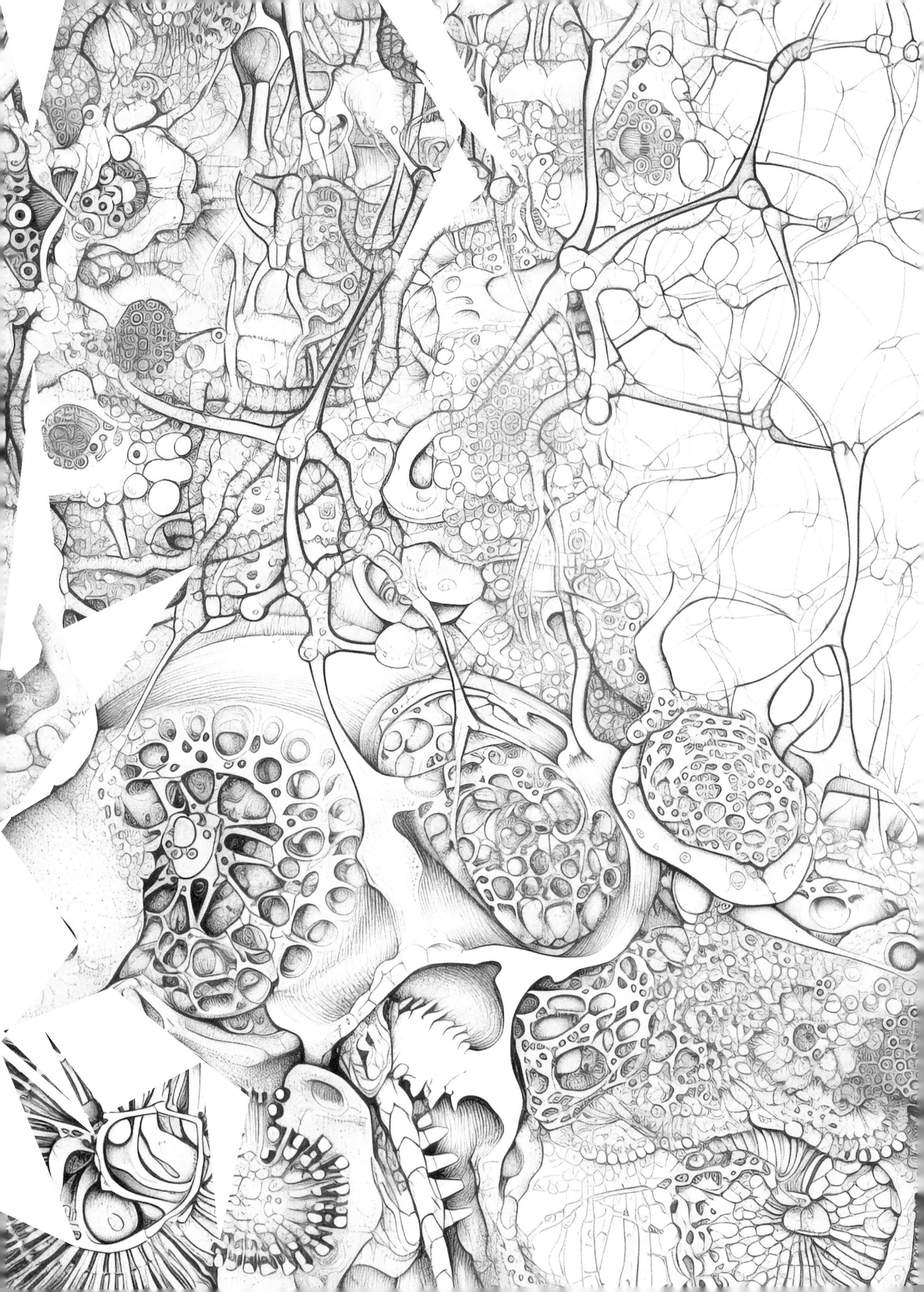

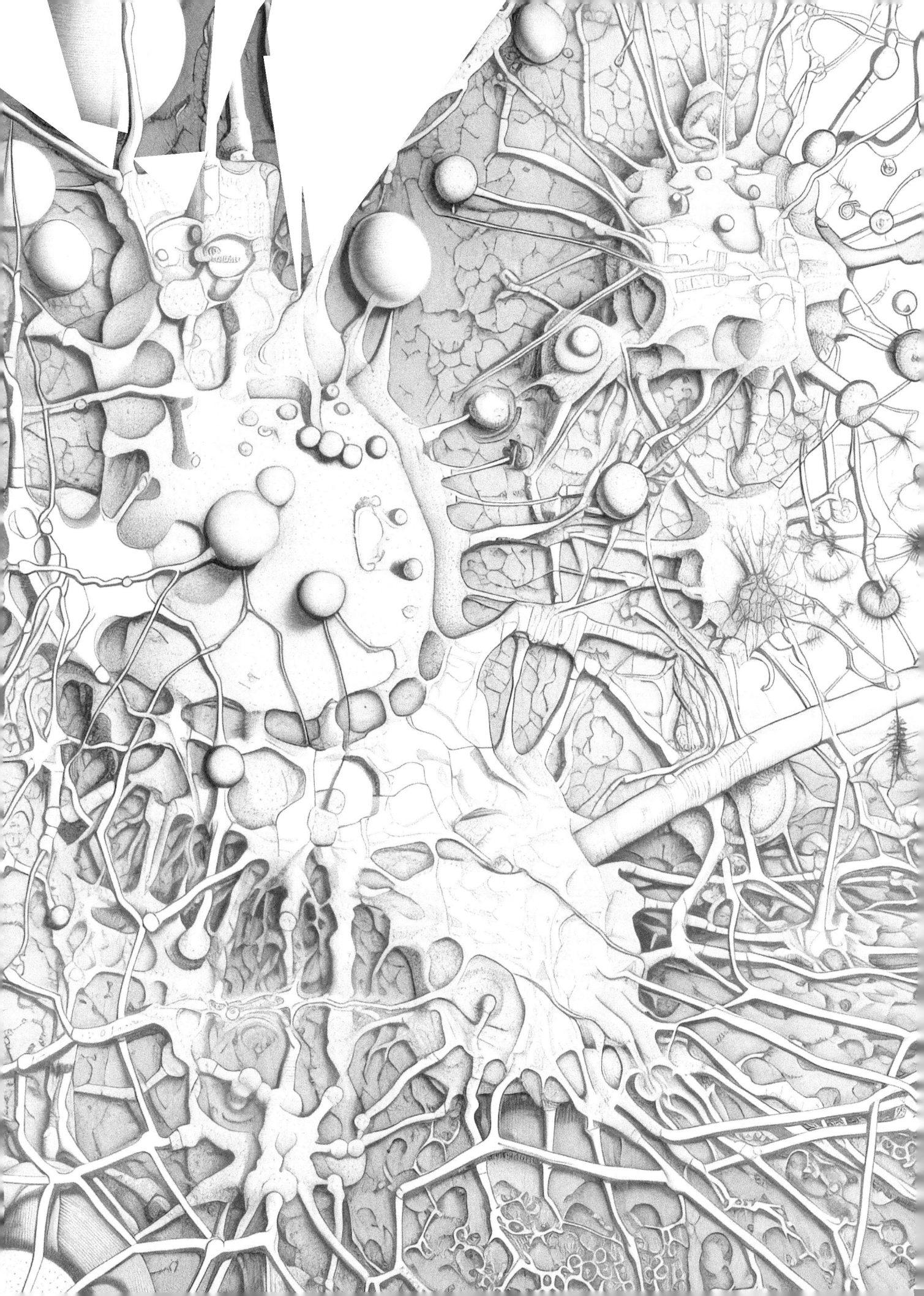

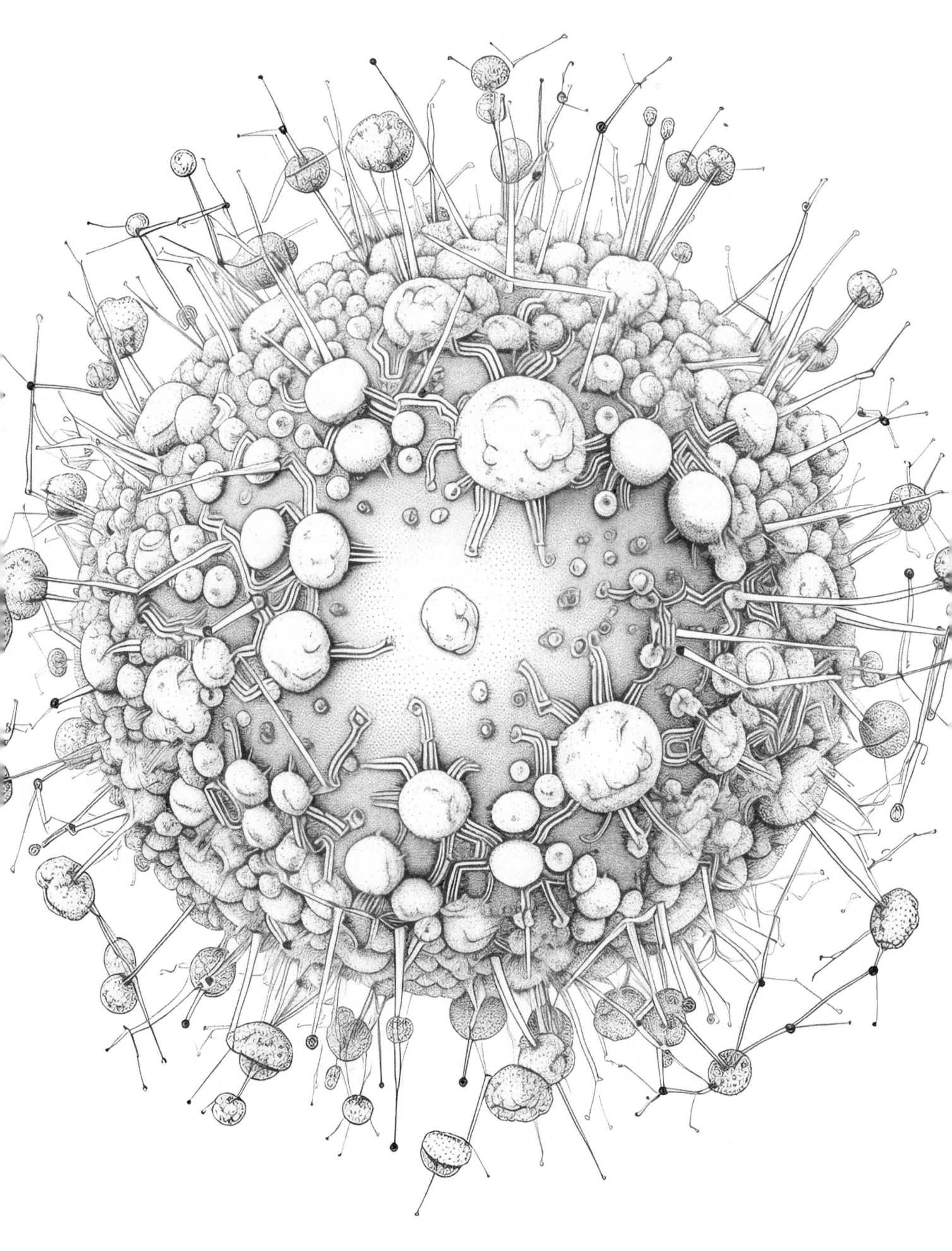

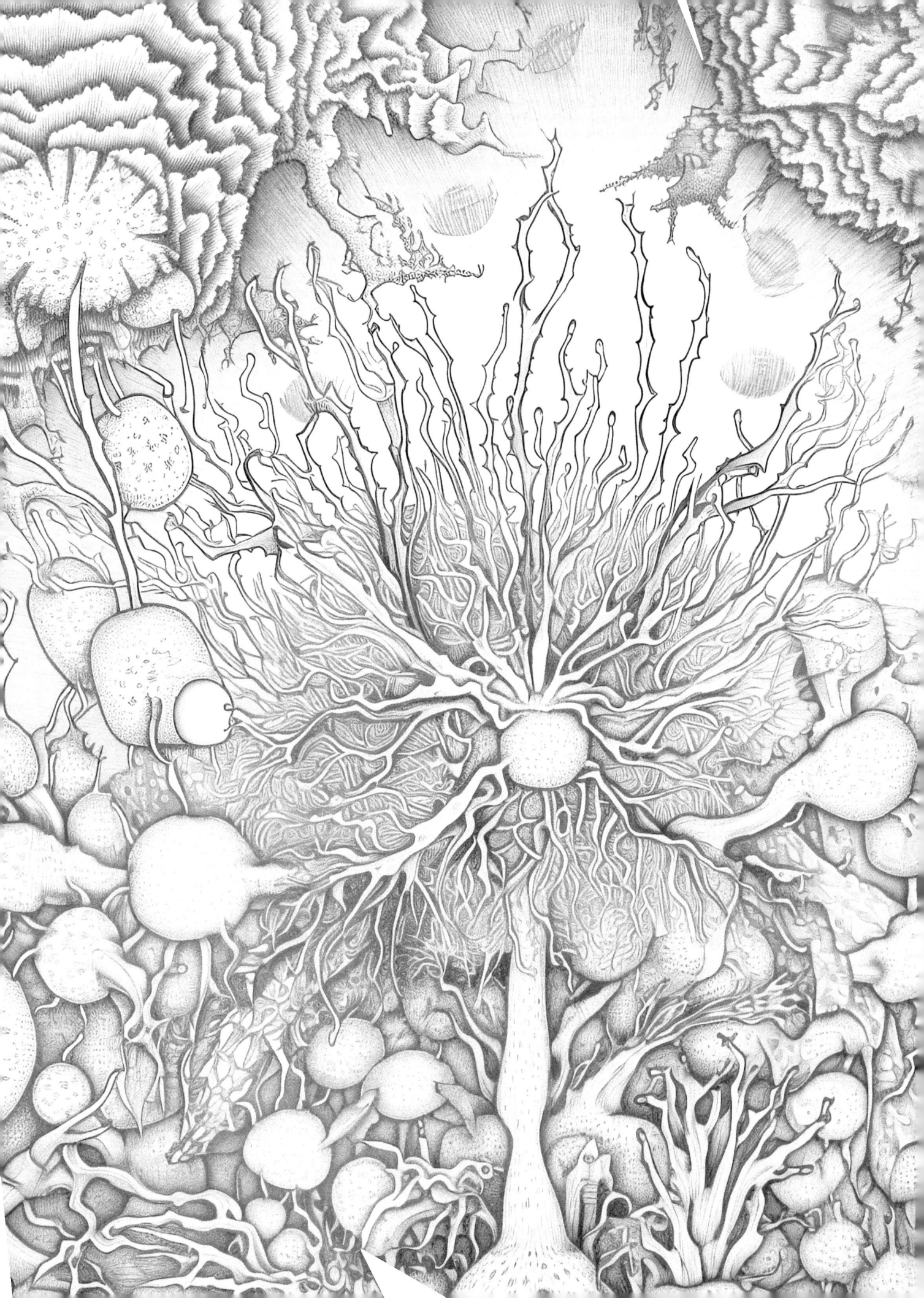

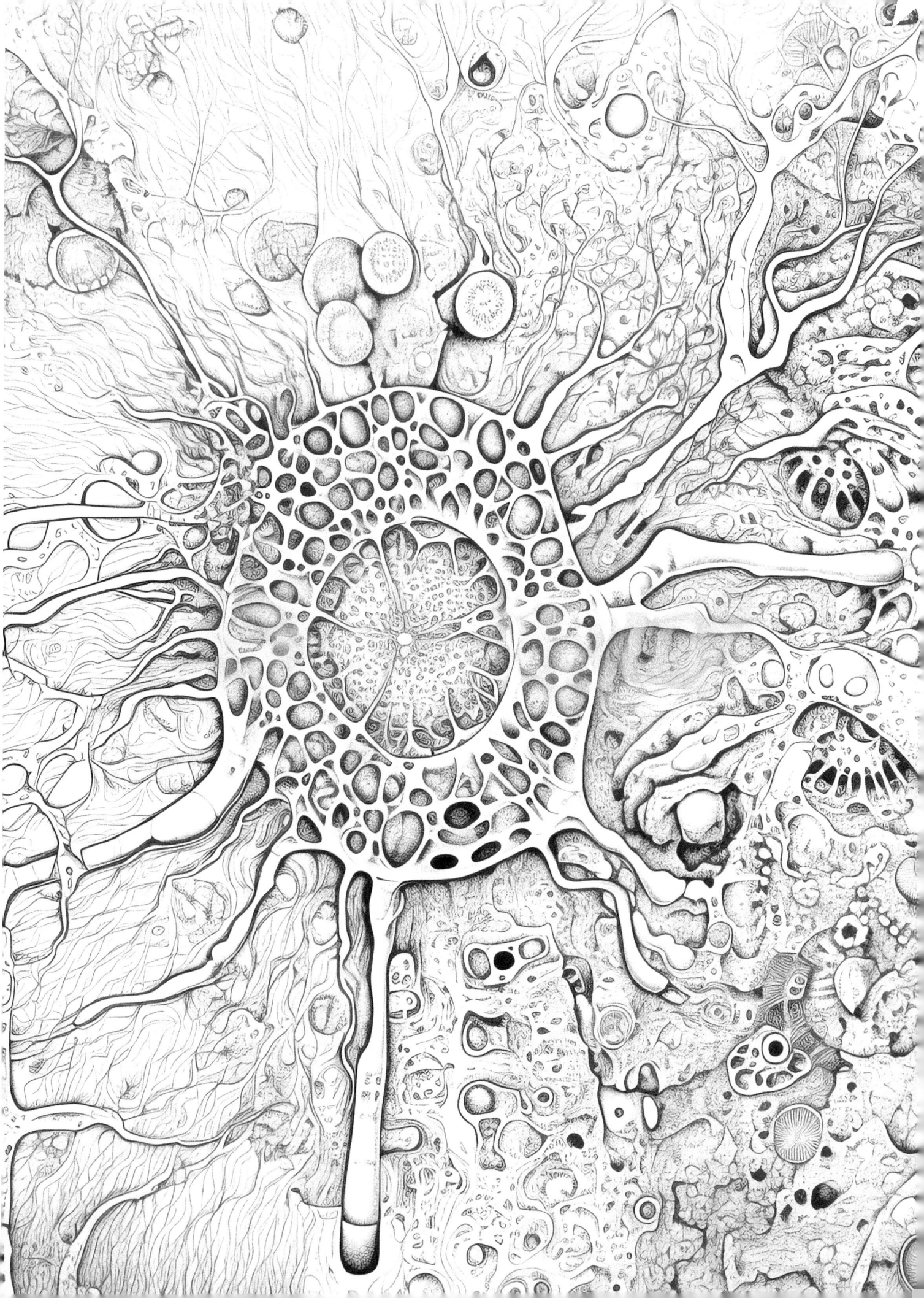

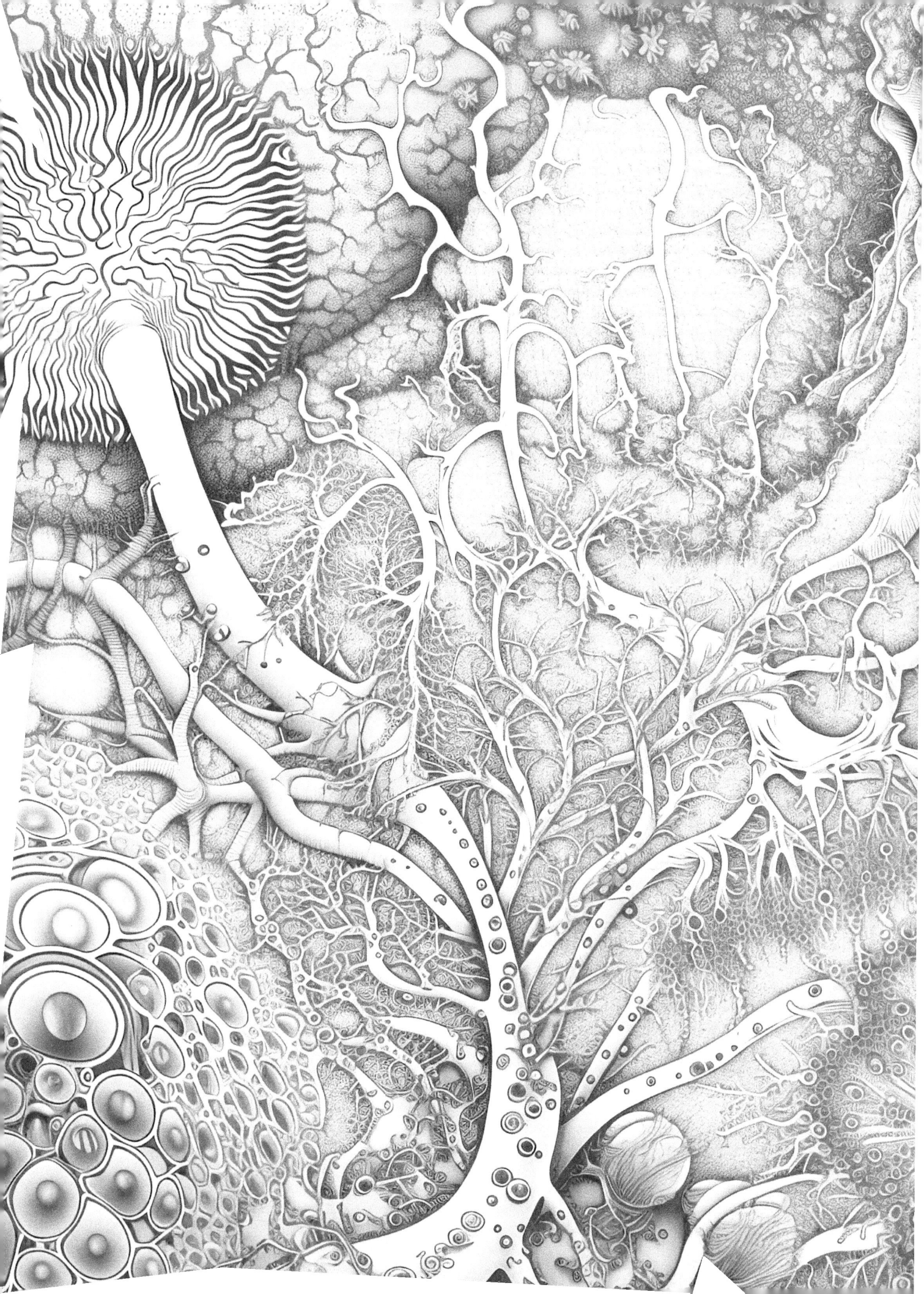

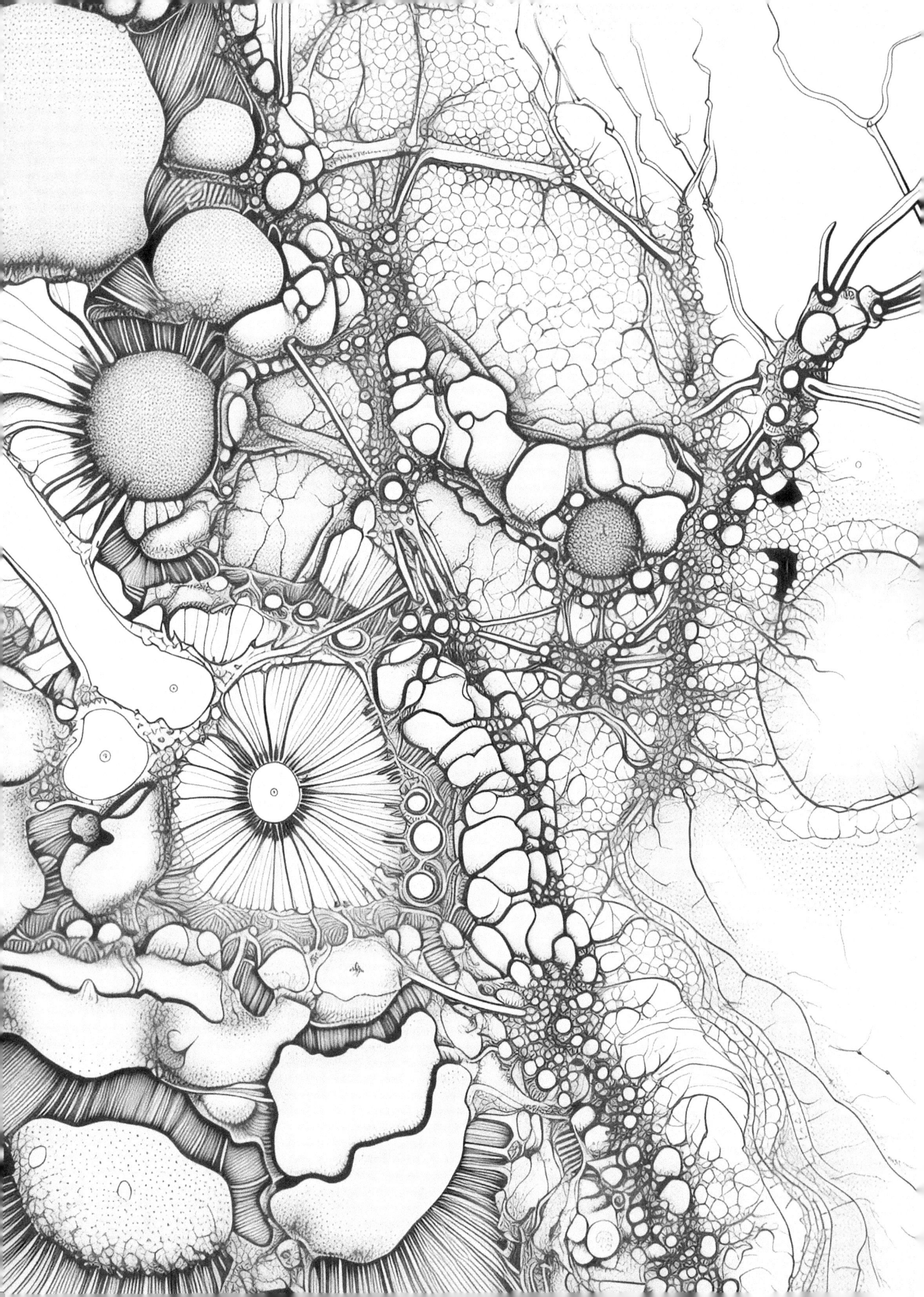

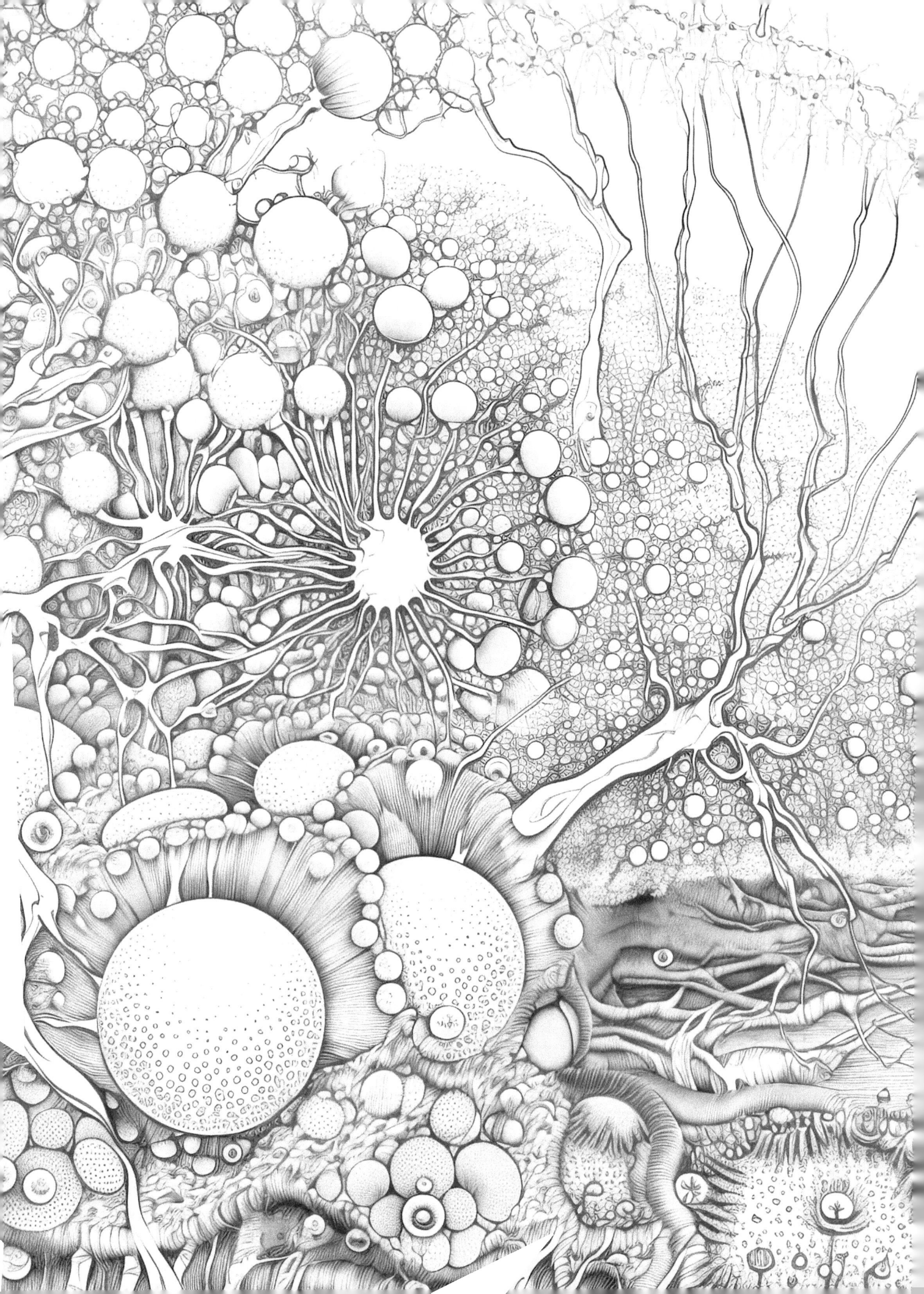

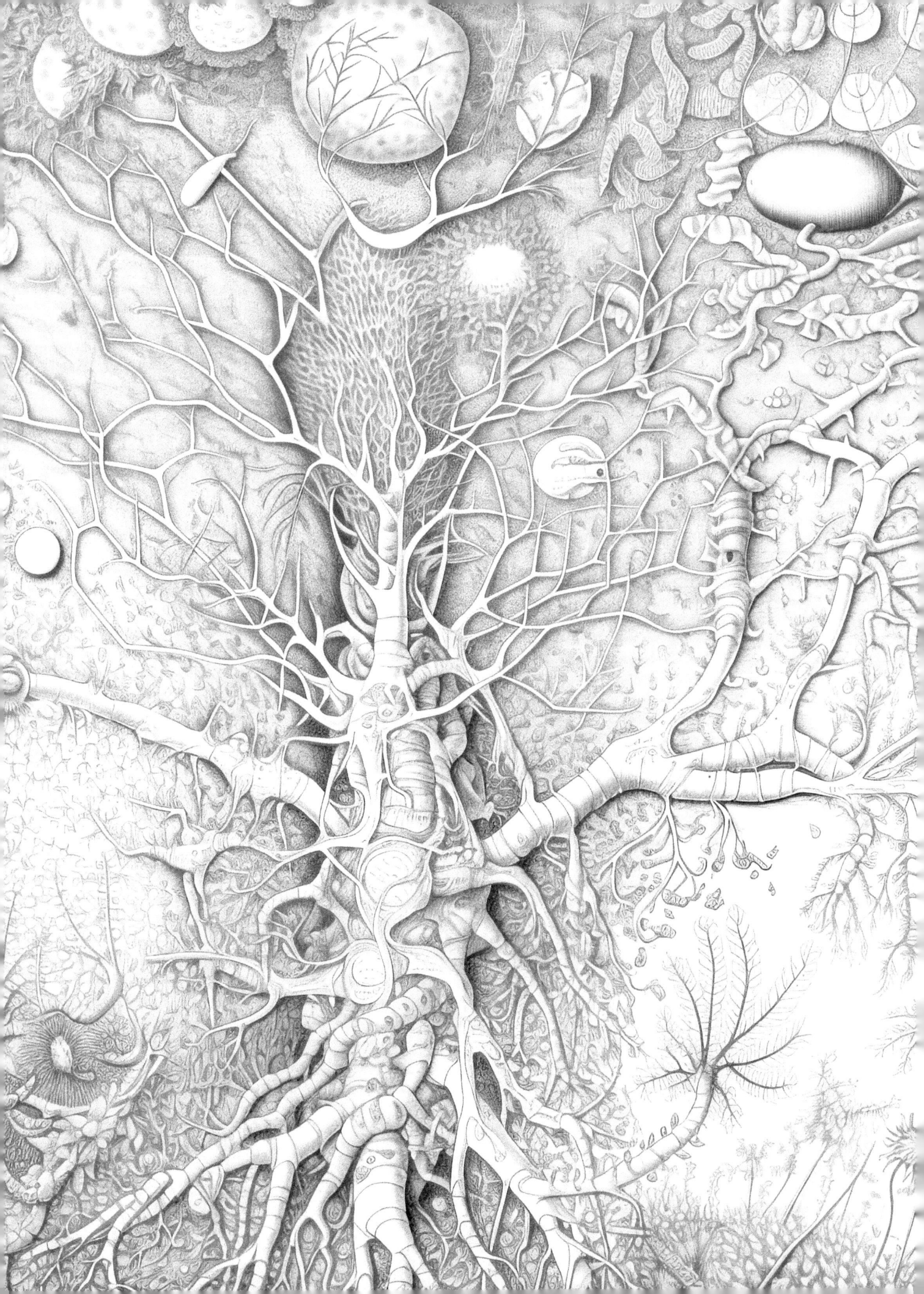

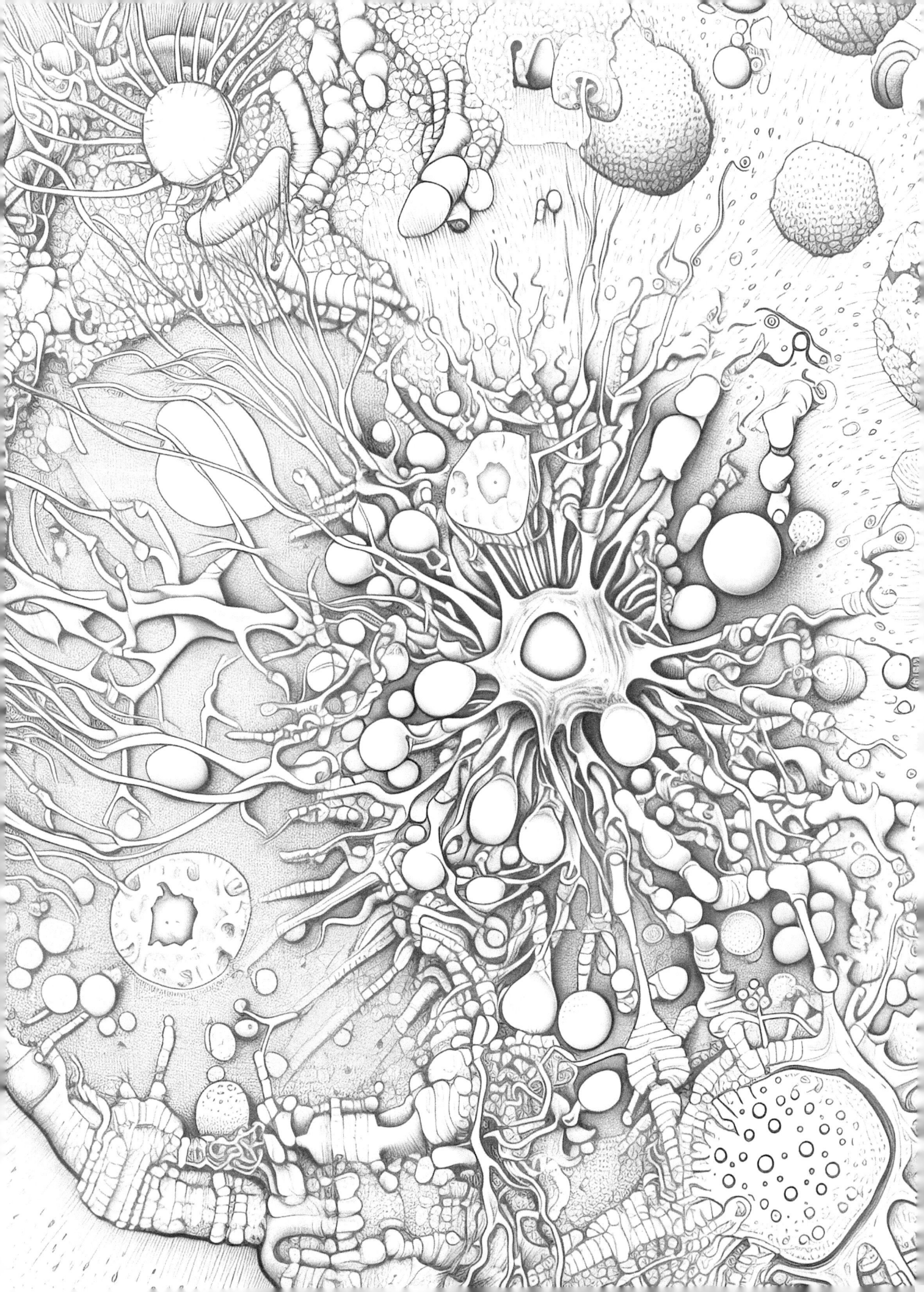

More Coloring Books from Antarctica Arts

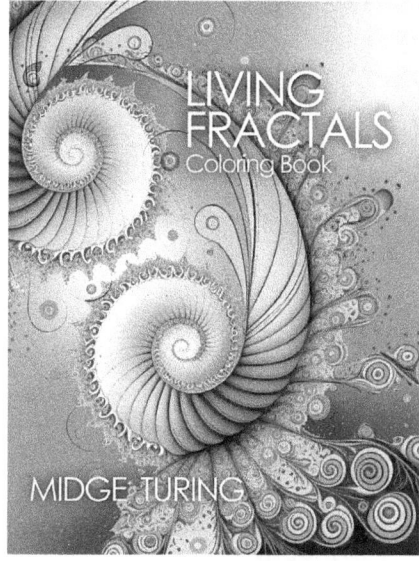
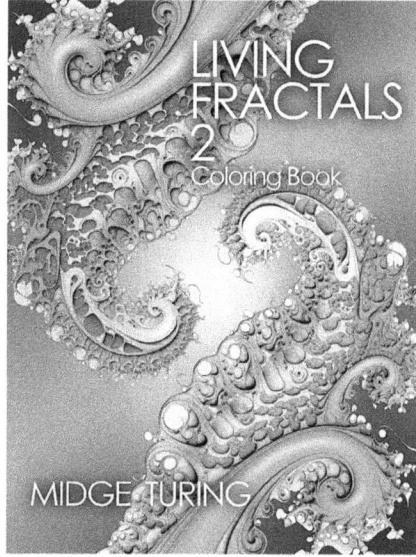
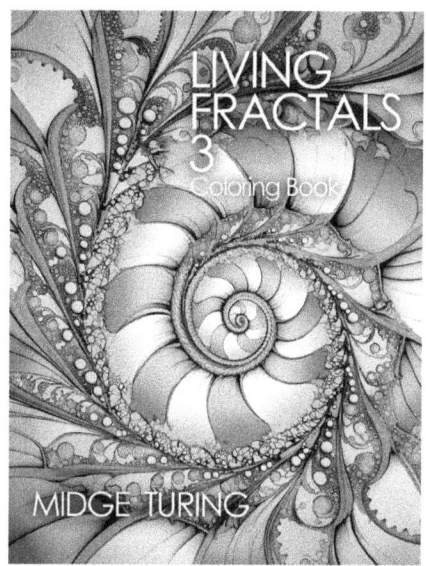
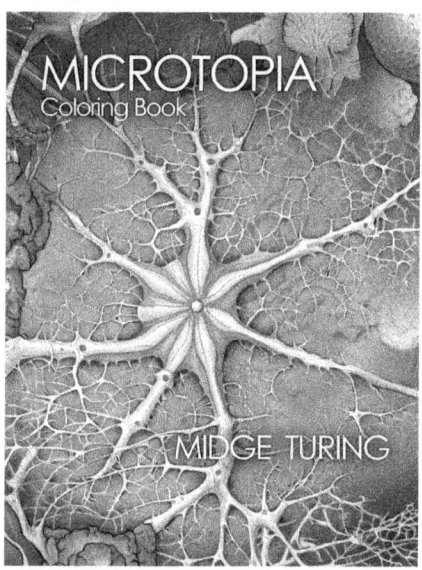

Want to color them again and again?
All coloring books are available as digital downloads on Etsy!
www.etsy.com/shop/antarcticaarts

www.ingramcontent.com/pod-product-compliance
Lightning Source LLC
Chambersburg PA
CBHW081347040426
42450CB00015B/3339